Digital Fashion Illustration
with Photoshop® and Illustrator®

DATE DUE

Digital Fashion Illustration with Photoshop® and Illustrator®

Kevin Tallon

BATSFORD

Thanks to all the contributors, especially those featured in the tutorials, for their efforts and help. Thanks to Fleur from Unit CMA for her great help on getting top illustrators. Thanks to Ronald and David for the photographs.

And finally a very special thanks to my wife Binia for putting up with the countless late nights and sparse quality time during the 6 months writing this book.

First published in the United Kingdom in 2008 by
Batsford
10 Southcombe Street
London W14 0RA

An imprint of Anova Books Company Ltd

ISBN−13 9780713490589

A CIP catalogue record for this book is available from the British Library.

15 14 13 12 11 10
10 9 8 7 6 5 4

Reproduction by Rival Colour Ltd, UK
Printed and bound by 1010 Printing International Ltd., China.

This book can be ordered direct from the publisher at the website:
www.anovabooks.com, or try your local bookshop

Distributed in the United States and Canada by Sterling Publishing Co.,
387 Park Avenue South, New York, NY 10016, USA

Front cover:
Mia Overgaard
Unmask me II

Back Cover:
Maren Esdar
Pantaloon-dress

Contents

Preface

Welcome to *Digital Fashion Illustration!*

Whether you are a fashion designer, an illustrator or you are simply curious to know how digital fashion illustrations are created, this book, I hope, should meet your expectations. *Digital Fashion Illustration* intends to bridge the gap between pure inspirational fashion illustration publications and digital-software user guides. My intention, in these pages, is to strike a balance between inspiration and information, between form and function.

Get inspired and learn

If you have read my previous book, *Creative Fashion Design with Illustrator*, you will notice how I have provided, in this new book, many more purely inspirational images with plenty of beautiful fashion illustrations. All the artworks have been arranged to follow and support the tutorials; they are visually inspiring so they will help you understand the tutorials better. Those step-by-step instructions annotated with a black background indicate corresponding artworks to illustrate the technique.

Pick and mix

I have arranged the skills required for each tutorial in chronological order from 'easy' to 'more difficult'. Early chapters are for beginners and later ones for more seasoned users, but adventurous readers can seek out specific tutorials to suit their needs regardless of their skill levels. I have had the chance to thoroughly 'road test' the best way to present information with fashion companies, students and evening-course attendees. The most important lesson I have learned from this hands-on testing period is how readers want to get to the specific skills they require without having to go through a whole tutorial. A sort of pick-and-mix modular approach to learning computer skills seems to be the preferred choice for most creative people. Quite often someone would need to go back to a particular skill over and over again, whereas other parts of a tutorial were assimilated swiftly. I have structured this new book in a less linear way, promoting selective browsing rather than reading from beginning to end. Each tutorial contains bite-sized chunks of skills to assimilate and any browser should be able to swiftly locate a required skill, easily finding exactly what he or she is looking for.

Skills are building blocks

I do not pretend that this new book is the be all and end all of digital fashion illustration but I have tried to cover as many illustrative styles and digital techniques as possible. Readers should be able to take out what they need and easily transpose acquired knowledge to their own creative work. The tutorials should serve as a starting point and help designers begin their work in context or at least be able to extrapolate some useful information for their own needs. One should look beyond the aesthetic value of any fashion illustration contained in this book, as what is most important for the reader is to assimilate the underlying skill and translate it into another illustrative context. The skills, tips and tricks presented in this book are building blocks from which to start developing your own fashion illustration.

Even though I have been a tireless advocate of all things digital I still believe that nothing can still quite match the simplicity and efficiency of a pen, brush or pencil to translate a designer's visual thought seamlessly into a sketch or illustration. Knowing how to draw freehand is still a prerequisite for most illustrators. Nevertheless, as digital design, enabled by more powerful and responsive hardware, becomes more and more 'natural', a new generation of 'digital artists' is emerging, capable of drawing freehand directly on the computer with either a mouse or graphics tablet. Several contributors to this book are working in such a way. They see a computer as nothing more than a sophisticated pencil or brush.

If you have never used a computer to produce fashion illustrations or have not used applications such as Illustrator or Photoshop to create fashion illustrations, then there has never been a better time to start. Powerful computers are now fairly cheap, digital creation is more and more common, and fashion illustration is enjoying a revival.

Kevin Tallon

Fashion illustration; a very brief history

Fashion illustration in its simplest expression is the representation of designed garments worn by a model. Its original purpose was to depict, as closely to reality as possible, how an outfit would look when worn. Fashion illustration has a rich history spanning over 500 years, within which countless events have occurred. It is not my intention to narrate them here; I will only focus on more recent history, which sets the context for the inception of digital illustration. Fashion illustration's evolution is closely linked to the development of new technologies and for better or worse, technology has strongly influenced how fashion illustration has been perceived over time.

The 1930s saw illustrated covers of Vogue magazine replaced by photography, making fashion illustration seemingly stuffy and old. As technology and progress drove through the century, fashion illustration's popularity kept on declining, remaining prevalent only in *haute-couture* circles and within specialized press publications such as WWD (*Womens Wear Daily*). However, seminal artists such as Antonio Lopez and Stephen Stipelman kept fashion illustration alive. Their efforts paid off with a strong revival of fashion illustration in the 1980s. But again, as the decade wore out and the excesses were all too clear to be seen, fashion illustration began to be seen as elitist over-indulgence.

Digital fashion illustration really started during the '90s as more affordable and capable technology made it possible for illustrators to experiment with this fledgling art form. Illustrators such as Jason Brooks revived fashion illustration in general and pioneered digital fashion illustration specifically by mixing freehand drawing skills with computer-generated vector graphics, delivering a fresh and stylish illustrative style iconic of the '90s.

Digital media; a very brief history too

The advent of the personal computer in the '80s can be described as the birth of the tool as far as digital fashion illustration is concerned. Mainframe computers were around since the late '50s but personal and affordable computers where a gigantic step closer to opening a world of possibilities for fashion illustrators. Nevertheless, budding digital artists would have to wait a long time for the gap to be bridged between clunky, hopelessly underpowered machines and million-colour multimedia ultra fast laptops.

Desktop computers then and now

As far as input devices were concerned, the advent of the mouse in the personal-computer market was another key milestone marked by the launch of the Apple Macintosh in 1984. Graphics tablets took much longer to migrate from high-end professional use to mainstream affordability due, without a doubt, to the fact that not everyone, even today, uses one; making the democratisation of this tool a much slower process. Desktop scanners, another key input device for digital illustrators, started to become available and more affordable around the early '90s and were crucial in enabling artists to digitize hand-drawn illustrations.

On the image-editing application side, a close relation between software and hardware evolution is much in evidence. The advent of innovative applications such as Adobe Photoshop in the early '90s was closely tied with the delivery of machines capable of supporting these kinds of software.

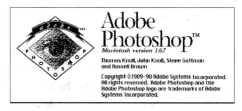

Adobe Photoshop 1.0.7 (1989)

Illustrator, for example, pushed the boundaries of screen size and greyscale depth to accommodate the software's advanced capabilities. Most importantly the advent of affordable image-editing software enabled illustrators to experiment and engage with their computer like never before.

The digital dawn

Fashion illustration has recently, regained momentum and interest from illustrators, publishers, readers and fashion companies alike. This new drive is firmly centred around editorial work and pure creativity since classical fashion illustration has long been superseded by the power and efficiency of slick fashion-production systems. This regained interest is probably due, in part, to the democratisation of accessible image-manipulation tools such as Adobe Photoshop and Illustrator and the explosion of media platforms from which any budding fashion illustrator can experiment. As aspects of media from web to traditional publishing and from blogs to digital portfolio have grown in size and number, so has the need for more visual content. Avid consumers of fashion trends but also adventurous art director have managed to re-energize the fashion-illustration scene. Computer cost, accessibility, speed and power (Moore's law tells us that computer power roughly doubles every 18 months) is also an important factor in making digital fashion illustration more accessible and user friendly.

Digital democracy

I have witnesses the rapid uptake of digital media in the fashion world first hand on many occasions and in different circumstances. The most telling of which was was when I started lecturing at Central Saint Martins in 2003 on the Menswear BA for a design project, which would become a regular yearly fixture in the curriculum. Back then a handful of students had a laptop computer, but as the project started again every year with a new cohort, the number of students with laptops steadily and gradually grew until it became an overwhelming majority, making 'laptopless' students virtual outcasts. Coupled to this, the computer's chip and graphic-card power kept on increasing, enabling students to manage much bigger files, experiment more freely, enjoy greater ease of use and explore new possibilities. This new generation of students and recent graduates 'born with a mobile phone in one hand and a mouse in the other' is already in evidence on the professional fashion scene; influencing with their unique values the whole design scene, from luminaries such as London designer Carrie Mundane to countless fashion illustrators shrewdly using social networking platforms such as Iqons or MySpace to promote their work online and across the globe.

Before starting

Quick overview

There are many tutorial-based books on the market explaining how to get the best out of different creative digital applications, but unfortunately they tend always to focus on non-fashion subjects. Historically there are certain kinds of users, such as graphic designers closely linked to the evolution of creative software applications, and they have been well catered for. Fashion illustrators and designers, on the other hand, have only recently become a critical mass requiring tailor-made books. This book is squarely aimed at people specifically wanting to design fashion illustration and nothing else.

How to get the most from this book

This book's tutorials have been developed with Adobe Photoshop and Illustrator. Both applications have huge breadth and depth (especially Photoshop), but I have tailored this book as far as possible for fashion illustrators and designers, avoiding irrelevant coverage of any tool, filter or technique and only focusing on what is useful.

Because it is impossible to cover every possible digital fashion-illustration technique, trick and skill, readers will have to do some lateral thinking and adapt basic techniques for their own needs. I have made the tutorials as short and sharp as possible, and as flexible as possible for anyone to adapt as they require. I have tried to avoid repeating skills, and thus each tutorial focuses on a specific skill set, which is a small part of the overall workflow. Readers will then need to pick and mix between tutorials to produce complete artworks. Usually, in each chapter, the first tutorial is easier than the second, and if any element or skill repeats from the first tutorial to the second they are quickly skimmed over. If you do not understand elements in the second tutorial try to go to the first one for more details.

Freehand drawing skills

I truly believe that freehand drawing skills are necessary and still relevant even in today's digital world. Nothing can make a bad freehand drawing better once digitized. Just as a bad digital photograph taken with a low-pixel mobile-phone camera can never be Photoshopped to become a picture of high quality, a bad freehand drawing cannot be Photoshopped to look good either. I care greatly about freehand drawing and lament that I do not have enough time to practise. I was lucky enough to be taught by Howard Tangye at Central Saint Martins. Postures, hands, faces, draping and textures, indeed every aspect of fashion illustration, were explored. I only later started working with computers to push further the boundaries of fashion illustration but never left behind freehand drawing. I strongly advise anyone seriously considering digital fashion illustration to first practise freehand drawing.

Positive attitude

There is no one fixed way of learning new computer skills, and every reader and budding digital artist will have different ways of assimilating and applying learned skills. This book is made for people who want to learn but also be inspired to create their own art and experiment for themselves. The tutorials are as flexible as possible so that readers can adapt and customize skills to suit their needs. If you have difficulties in assimilating skills, I suggest that you drill down on fewer elements until you are able to do them as unconsciously as possible. There is nothing more rewarding than to be able to do a complicated operation seamlessly and without having to refer to any book or tutorial. People who fear computers or have negative perceptions of their own potentials are always worst off. Go through this book, be positive and, most importantly, enjoy it. Be patient: you will never be able to learn everything overnight. Be humble: only your real skills will define your art.

Copyright issues

Quite often digital artists will use catwalk pictures, fashion adverts and other visual sources as templates to trace from; this is fine as long as your artwork is substantially different from the original image. Usually 70 per cent of modification should be evident. Although this can be quite hard to estimate without being a copyright expert, common sense prevails. As long as the original image is not instantly recognisable, and you have changed enough features, such as background, medium, colours etc., you should be fine. With today's technology you can take a picture of a friend in the pose you require and use it as a dummy template onto which you can draw and compose fantastic fashion illustrations.

Mac vs PC

Is the Mac vs PC debate still relevant? Convergence is upon us and working from one platform to the other has never been as easy. Adobe applications were originally developed for the Mac but now things are pretty even. This book's tutorials have been designed on the Mac and therefore all screen grabs are Mac generated. However, PC users should feel confident that they can use the book as easily as Mac users.

Which applications?

The main applications used to develop the step-by-step tutorials and by most contributors are Adobe Photoshop and Illustrator. Both these applications are the industry standard for fashion illustrators. Macromedia Freehand was killed off by Adobe when the company took over Macromedia. There are other applications, such as Corel Draw and Painter, which some digital artists use frequently. Corel Draw is a PC-only application and therefore not used by a majority of designers working on Macs, while Painter is mainly used by digital artists working in animation and fantasy illustration.

Adobe CS3

This book covers Adobe Photoshop and Illustrator CS3, which were released in the spring of 2007. Users of earlier versions should have no problems in following the tutorials, although I recommend having at least Photoshop and Illustrator CS2, especially with regards to Illustrator's Live Trace tool, which started with CS2. If any features are specific to a version of Illustrator only they will be clearly indicated as such.

Keyboard shortcuts

Readers should as much as possible use keyboard shortcuts; they help you work faster and with both hands. Each tutorial will include both Mac and PC keyboard shortcuts. The main difference between Mac and PC keyboards is when using modifier keys: the Mac uses the Command key and the PC the Control key. For example, to create a new file Mac users will use Command + O and PC users Control + O. To avoid lengthy tutorial copy, I have displayed only the most common symbol or abbreviation found on both Mac and PC keyboards. Here is a list of symbols and abbreviations used throughout the book and their equivalent.

Symbols and abbreviations	Equivalent
Ctrl	Control key
⌘ or ⌘ (Mac only)	Command key
Alt or ⌥	Alt key
↑	Shift key

Quick tips

'Quick tips' highlight key skills or issues that demand special attention; they usually help the reader understand in more depth a tutorial, a given skill or a particularly difficult aspect of a tutorial. Quick tips offer an insider's knowledge on invaluable skills and techniques that would normally take months to grasp when self-taught. I have encountered, on countless occasions, advanced digital artists with years of experience doing things either the long or the wrong way. A good tip can dramatically change your productivity and enhance your experience when designing on the computer. Look out for them!

Adobe Photoshop CS3 Icon

Adobe Illustrator CS3 Icon

Digital illustration workflow

Workflow describes the way in which you, as a digital artist, are going to manage your creative output from initial concept to final delivery. Any prolific digital fashion illustrator should have a tailor-made workflow enabling him to save time and turn around any artwork efficiently, leaving as much time as possible to creativity and dedicating as little time as possible to repetitive tasks and processes. Because each designer works differently it is impossible to have a 'one size fits all' workflow. Nevertheless, there are commonalities, which can apply more or less to all digital artists. Below are the key stages, which a digital fashion illustration should go through:

1 **Source:** Fashion illustration workflow usually starts with the artist drawing an illustration or sourcing a suitable image to be used as a template to trace on to digitally. The more time spent at this stage, in terms of the quality of the template image or freehand drawing, the less time spent at the pre-production stage.
2 **Input:** At this stage, the freehand drawing will be scanned in, the source image uploaded from a digital camera, downloaded from the web or scanned from a magazine. As a rule of thumb, for print output, scan at 300dpi; for images from the web try to source file size above 500K to avoid pixelation.

3 **Pre-production:** This stage concerns only digital artists working with a template to draw their illustration on the computer and can range from slight adjustment to heavy pre-production such as compositing various images into one to get the best template possible for your needs.
4 **Production:** Again this workflow stage is for the digital fashion illustrator composing on the computer directly, although the template on which the production will occur can also include freehand drawings onto which digital effects or textures will be added later.
5 **Post-production:** An illustration mainly composed outside the computer is scanned and retouched to eliminate minor elements such as smudges and blemishes. It is also usually colour corrected and balanced.
6 **Back-up and archiving:** Completed digital illustrations should be saved first in native Photoshop or Illustrator format to retain an original and editable file. Making an extra safe copy for archiving on a back-up device other than your computer is thoroughly recommended.
7 **Output:** Depending on how the illustration will be outputted, different file formats and sizes should be used: for email or web, save as JPEG at 72dpi (Photoshop) or PDF format (Illustrator). For print, save as TIFF format at 300dpi.

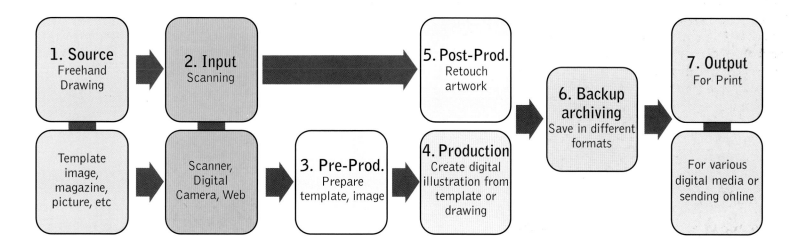

Digital tools

Digital artists need much more than a sketchpad and a pencil box to get up and running. If you can afford it, try to invest in good-quality hardware. This will always pay for itself over time, as better equipment tends to be more reliable and last longer. Here is a quick overview of the key hardware tools necessary to produce digital fashion illustrations.

Computer: Either PC or Mac as long as there is plenty of RAM (2GB) and generous hard-drive space (200GB). Laptops are popular but are more expensive, with lower specs, and they tend to break down more often. A bigger screen is useful for viewing comfort, although not essential.

Scanner: A decent mid-priced scanner should satisfy most digital fashion illustrators for day-to-day scanning. High-end scanners are extremely expensive, so if you seldom require high-quality scanning, use a reprographic house, which will charge per scan.

Graphics tablet: A very useful input device, especially for digital painting. Quality tablets with larger surfaces are worth investing in as they are more precise and pressure sensitive, making the digital freehand-drawing experience much more natural, convincing and enjoyable.

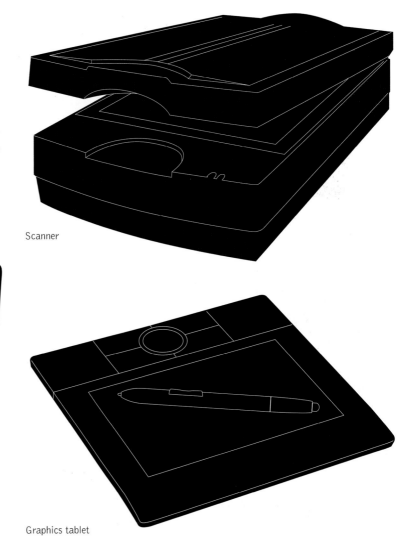

Scanner

Computer

Graphics tablet

Digital camera: A good digital camera will save you time and effort when retouching pictures. Don't believe the pixel hype above and beyond 4 megapixels. What really makes a good digital camera is its lenses and the quality of the CCD chip. Phones are quickly catching up with decent inbuilt cameras and are always with you, and can be a great tool for inspiration snapshots.

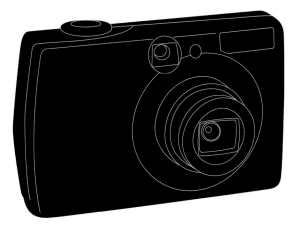

Digital camera

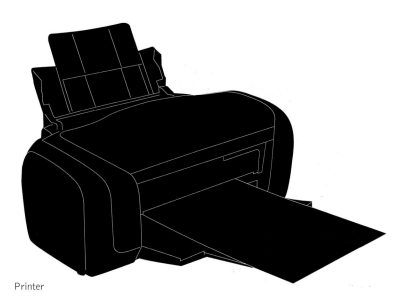

Printer

Printer: Although digital content represented on screen is becoming all-encompassing, the tactile nature and timelessness of printed matter still makes owning a printer essential. Good ink-jet printers are able to display vivid colours and flawless solid-fill areas. If you can afford it, go for oversize A3 for more impact.

External hard drive: Digital media has its drawbacks, namely the ease with which a file can be lost forever, from an accidental deletion to a computer breakdown. It is wise to make safe back-up copies on an external hard drive, which can be securely stowed away. External hard drives offer the advantage of being relatively affordable and able to read and write large files rapidly; they also last longer than DVDs or CDs.

Following the trend of ever-increasing power, miniaturization and innovation, digital artist's tools are set to carry on evolving. This should make them yet more intuitive and less cumbersome. Prices should also carry on falling, making digital tools more affordable and accessible to all.

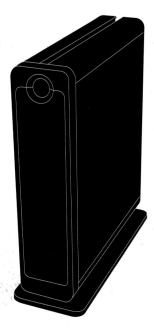

External hard drive

Adobe Photoshop

Basic principles

This book is not intended as a fully fledged instruction manual for Photoshop. However, below is a quick-start overview of the application's key features and tools most relevant to fashion illustrators.

Photoshop is bitmap image manipulation software; any image created or edited in Photoshop is made of pixels. The more pixels, the better the image quality.

Image resolution describes how many pixels are contained within a given image's size. Both images below are of the same size (5 x 6cm/ 2 x 2⅜in) but the one on the left has a resolution of 72dpi (dots per inch), whereas the one on the right contains over four times more pixels at 300dpi.

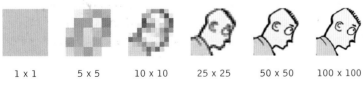

| 1 x 1 | 5 x 5 | 10 x 10 | 25 x 25 | 50 x 50 | 100 x 100 |

A 72dpi image 142 x 212 pixels
© Ronald Dick

The same image at 300dpi (591 x 885 pixels)

The interface

Photoshop's depth and power has dramatically evolved over its 17-year history; on the other hand, apart from a few graphic enhancements and tweaks Photoshop CS3's interface remains very similar to the original version. Getting to know Photoshop's interface key elements will help novice users navigate and feel more at ease with the application.

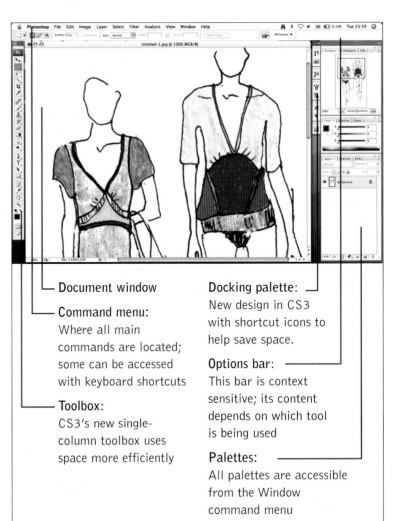

Document window

Command menu:
Where all main commands are located; some can be accessed with keyboard shortcuts

Toolbox:
CS3's new single-column toolbox uses space more efficiently

Docking palette:
New design in CS3 with shortcut icons to help save space.

Options bar:
This bar is context sensitive; its content depends on which tool is being used

Palettes:
All palettes are accessible from the Window command menu

Main features

Essentially, for most digital fashion illustrators, Photoshop consists of three main areas: image correction and retouching; image manipulation and composition; and digital painting. Each of these areas has dedicated menu commands, tools and palettes. Photoshop's depth and scope is vast, so only the most commonly used functions and tools are highlighted below for each area.

Image correction and retouching

When scanning an illustration or opening a digital image, the usual first step is to correct its contrast, level and colour. All these can be found under Menu > Image > Adjustment. Most commonly used adjustments are **Levels** and **Saturation**, but also **Shadow Highlight**, **Brightness/Contrast** and **Curves**. Only experience and practice can make a digital artist fluent in using these various adjustments. Image correction is very useful when suppressing a freehand drawing's stains and blemishes.

   Retouching an image is an important skill, especially for artworks mainly created outside digital applications. Various tools such as the **Eraser,** the **Clone tool** and the **Healing Brush tool** can, once mastered, easily get rid of paper creases and blemishes. Some filters, such as **Dust and Scratches** and **Reduce Noise** are also useful: they can be found under Menu > Filter > Noise.

Image manipulation and composition

For digital artists keen to exploit and bridge the gap between hand-drawn and digitally produced illustrations, image manipulation is an important feature of Photoshop. Menu > Filter > Filter Gallery... brings countless options of eye-catching **filter effects** on any scanned illustration. Photoshop's **layers** are vital when compositing and manipulating any image and **Blending modes** make layers interact with each other. To be able to manipulate an image properly, an illustrator needs various selection tools, either to work on a specific area of the image or to cut and paste it into a new layer with tools such as the **Marquee, Magic Wand** and **Lasso.**

Digital painting

This key area of Photoshop is for illustrators mainly working on the computer, often using rough freehand sketches as a template on which to paint. Any serious digital painter should invest into a good graphics tablet to make digital painting as close to real painting as possible. The brush is the main tool used for digital painting; it is highly customizable and like any other elements in Photoshop works really well with layers and blending modes.

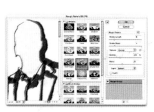

Filter Gallery: use with moderation since preset filters can look quite obvious and tacky

Marquee, Quick selection and Lasso tools

The Layer palette is essential for image compositing; note the Blending mode pop-down menu on the top-left corner

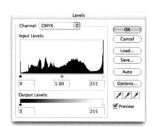

The Level palette: very useful when preparing a scanned black pen illustration for colouring

The Dust and Scratch filter helps to clean up a scanned image

Heal, Clone and Eraser tools

The Brush palette

Brush tool

Adobe Illustrator

Basic principles

Adobe Illustrator has come a long way since its first inception in 1986; it is now a de facto industry standard with which most illustrators work and create.

Illustrator is a vector-based application. Vector graphics, unlike bitmap, can be scaled up without losing quality. There is no such thing as pixelation on images created with Illustrator's vector tools.

Mixed media

One key feature of Illustrator is that the application can also support and display bitmap graphics, making Illustrator a very versatile application, which can be used to draw and paint but also layout images alongside vector-generated graphics.

Even at close-up range, drawn lines remain crisp and sharp

This illustration mixes a scanned freehand drawing with added vector detailing produced in Illustrator

The interface

Illustrator's interface has constantly evolved to reflect and adapt to the demanding needs of digital artists. CS3's new interface, like Photoshop, focuses on saving as much space as possible for the artwork window, thus minimizing the size and footprint of floating palettes. Interestingly, Illustrator's interface has come closer to Photoshop for obvious cross-application consistency. Below are the main areas making up Illustrator's interface.

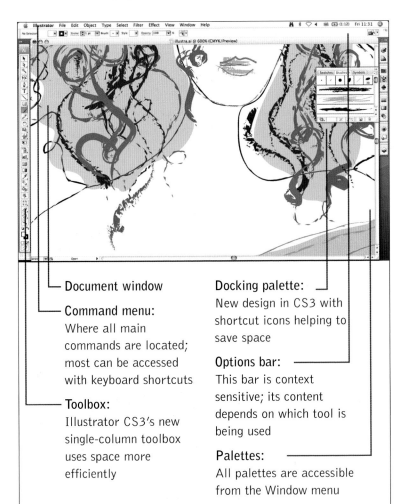

Document window

Command menu:
Where all main commands are located; most can be accessed with keyboard shortcuts

Toolbox:
Illustrator CS3's new single-column toolbox uses space more efficiently

Docking palette:
New design in CS3 with shortcut icons helping to save space

Options bar:
This bar is context sensitive; its content depends on which tool is being used

Palettes:
All palettes are accessible from the Window menu

Main features

Originally, vector graphics mainly consisted of slick lines and solid colours, but today Illustrator features, among other things, gradients, 3-D effects and Photoshop-like filters. The application contains several key features and tools for digital fashion illustrators, which can be broadly divided in three areas: **Tracing, Composition** and **Vector painting.**

Tracing

When a scanned freehand sketch or a digital image is opened in Illustrator, it can be used as a template to trace onto (Illustrator handles most bitmap image formats: JPEG, Photoshop, TIFF, etc.). The first step is to lock the image layer and then create a new one on which to trace using either the **Pen** (more precise) or **Pencil** tool (similar to freehand). Tracing is quite a straightforward process but a few basic rules apply: 1. always try to create a closed shape and 2. create a layer for each key area of your tracing (silhouette, garments, body features, etc.).

Live Tracing is a new and powerful feature since Illustrator CS2 and enables automatic tracing and conversion to vectors of any bitmap image. Unfortunately, Live Tracing can be unwieldy and create over-complicated objects. For best results, make sure your scanned image is as clean and as simple as possible with uniform colour areas.

Composition

Illustrator's media versatility makes it very good at creating composite illustration layouts using a mixture of pictures, text and vector graphics, which are easier to edit and modify than in Photoshop. Any fashion illustration created in Illustrator using vector tools such as the Pen can be relatively easily modified and re-coloured, have its background picture changed etc. The Text tool is also more versatile and interactive in Illustrator. The interaction between the different media can be further enhanced using the Transparency palette's **Blending modes** (Menu > Window > Transparency).

Vector painting

Illustrator's paintbrush is the main tool used to create freehand vector painting; its killer feature is the fact that it can be modified on the fly once a brush stroke is made, to alter its appearance radically, changing, for example, from rough ink to a slick calligraphic brush. Any vector object created in Illustrator can have a brush applied to it and any vector object can also be transformed into a brush.

Using the Pencil tool, the image on the left and right have the same traced vector objects (the hair and the T-shirt) but they have different brushes (hair) and different blending modes (T-shirt), which substantially changes the illustration appearance

The tracing on the left is open at the neck and the centre front, which makes the fill colour 'spill out' of the coat. The one on the right is a closed shape (all of its segment and anchor points are seamlessly attached, keeping the fill colour in)

The picture on the right has been live traced using the Detailed Illustration preset found in the control palette's Live Trace pop-up menu

The Pen and Pencil tool

Chapter 1
Scanning and retouching illustrations

This chapter focuses on how to scan, clean up, retouch and colour correct original artworks in both black and white and colour in regular and oversized formats.

The first step for anyone, from novice to seasoned digital fashion illustrator, is to convert artwork from analogue to digital format, from pencil to pixel. As highlighted in the Digital Illustration Workflow, page 11, this can either be done with a scanner or a digital camera. This chapter contains mainly artworks, which are entirely developed without the aid of a computer, but subsequently digitized to be slightly retouched, colour corrected or cleaned up. Artists who are happy to work with natural media, but wish to, for example, email or post their artworks on a website would greatly benefit from going through the tutorials to gain understanding on how to achieve results on scanned images quickly.

Tutorial highlights

Tutorial 1
This is for those who draw mainly sketches in black and white with lots of pencil marks and stained paper and need to either clean up or prepare for digital colouring.

Tutorial 2
If you have large-scale artworks needing to be scanned in several parts, look into this tutorial. Also, you will find more tips on cleaning up and retouching.

Tutorial 3
When you work on very large formats and prefer to take a snapshot digital picture and then need to colour correct and adjust the image, please follow this tutorial.

Tutorial 4
This final tutorial looks at how to deal with textured artworks containing spots and stains needing more advanced retouching skills using the Clone Stamp tool and the Healing Brush tool.

Key skills:	Application:	Key tools:	Key menu functions:
Scanning	Photoshop	Crop tool	Menu > Image > Adjustment > Levels or Brightness/Contrast
Image and colour correction		Clone tool	or Curves
Cleaning up a scanned drawing		Healing Brush tool	
Retouching blemishes and marks		Eraser tool	
Colour and area selection		Lasso tool	

Danny Roberts, The Posse.
Black felt-tip pen, Photoshop

Lovisa Burfitt,
Mini.
Brush with ink, steel-feather pen
with ink, pencil, thin felt-tip pen,
coloured pencils, Photoshop

Lovisa Burfitt,
Konitchiwa!
Brush with ink, steel-feather pen
with ink, coloured pencils,
Photoshop

Tutorial 1

Scanning and cleaning up a freehand sketch

Quite often freehand sketches are done quickly and traced with a pen on top of pencilled templates; add to this eraser marks, crumpled paper and white correcting pen and you get a pretty messy illustration ready to be scanned.

1 Don't worry about trying to clean up the mess on your illustration with more erasing and white pen; simply place the image on your scanner, making sure it is as straight as possible and that the paper is nice and flat. Close the scanner cover and launch Photoshop.

2 Go to File > Import > (there you should see your scanner listed) select your scanner. Select Preview in the scanner's interface window then, using the Marquee tool, frame your illustration preview leaving a bit of space around the edges. For good-quality scans, for print output, select 300dpi. Finish by clicking on the scan button.

3 Go back to Photoshop by closing the scanner window. The first step is to adjust the contrast of the scan, trying to make the white pure white and the black deep black. Work with Levels: Menu > Image > Adjustment > Levels (⌘ + L Mac or Ctrl + L for Windows PC).

4 The key here is to move the black-and-white sliders towards the centre to alter the levels without losing image definition (press the Alt key while doing this to visualize how many pixels are 'clipped', i.e. lost). Use the Eyedropper tool found on the lower right side, select the black one then click on the darkest pixel found on the scan, repeat with white, selecting the lightest pixel.

5 The image should start looking more like a black-pen drawing on pure white paper. You will not manage to get rid of all the stains, especially when wanting to keep the integrity of the scan. Again, the key is not to lose too much definition by overdoing the Levels.

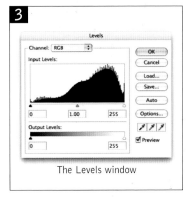

The original scan

The Levels window

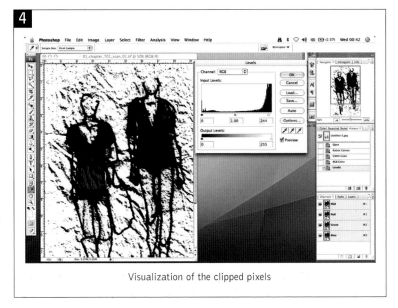

Visualization of the clipped pixels

6

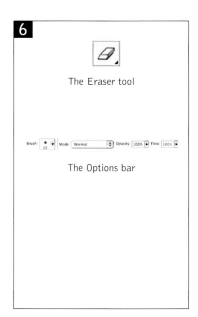

The Eraser tool

The Options bar

The scan half-way
through cleaning

7

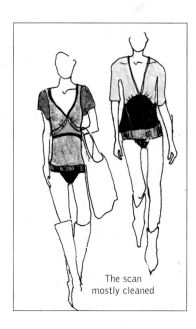

The Polygonal Lasso tool

The brush size contextual menu
(when the eraser is set to Brush in
the Options bar, right click on the
canvas to open this menu)

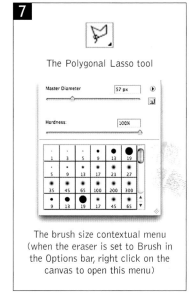

The scan
mostly cleaned

6 Use the Eraser tool set to Paintbrush to erase the remaining stains around the illustration. Make sure your background colour is set to white to re-create pure white paper. Use a big brush to work faster.

7 With a smaller brush, get closer to the edge of the illustration and chip away stains closer to the edge of the drawn line, making sure you do not touch the black outline stroke of the drawing. You can also use the Polygonal Lasso tool to select around the illustration by 'lassoing' the stains away.

8 Press (⌘ + Alt + 0 or Ctrl + 0 for Windows PC) or go to Menu > View > Actual Pixels. This brings you to the best view before the image starts pixelating. Using the Eraser and the Lasso, delete the remaining stains.

9 To finish cleaning up, use the eraser to get rid of any drawn mistakes, such as on the left arm of the illustration, top right. You can also use a brush to paint missing lines, making sure you select a soft-edge brush with the right diameter.

8

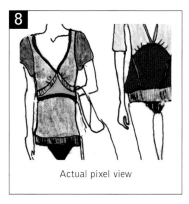

Actual pixel view

9

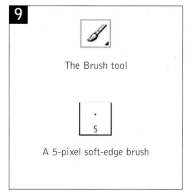

The Brush tool

A 5-pixel soft-edge brush

■ Quick tip

Scan your illustration in colour mode even if you have only used black-and-white media; this helps the scanner in picking up more subtleties and gradients. Once scanned, revert to Grayscale mode: Menu > Image > Mode > Grayscale.

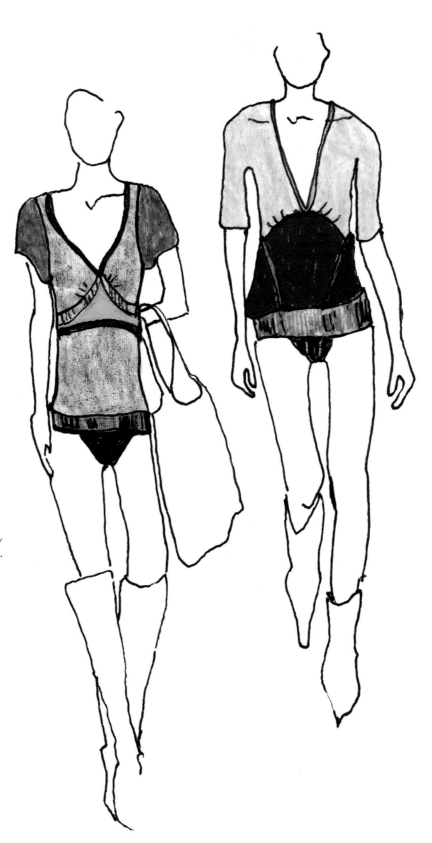

Binia Umland,
Collection Sketches.

Ploi Horwang,
The Look.
Coloured pencils, Photoshop

Am I Collective,
Hair.
Ink, pencil, Photoshop

Tutorial 2

Scanning and cleaning up large-scale illustrations

Large-scale scanners are expensive and knowing how to scan and compose seamlessly anything bigger than an A4 sheet onto regular-sized scanners is an invaluable skill. Moving on from the first tutorial, more cleaning up and retouching skills on freehand drawn illustrations are explored.

1   Start as in Tutorial 1 by scanning your illustration using Photoshop's import function. Visualize where is the best place to position the artwork within your scanner's flatbed area to minimize the number of scans required to digitize your entire artwork. It might be useful to take off your scanner's cover to avoid folding the artwork's paper.

2   After positioning your first portion of artwork on the scanner, remind yourself where the drawing reaches the edge of the flatbed scanning area. It is important to make sure that at least one of your artwork edges is flush and parallel with the scanning area's side rulers.

3   Once the first portion is scanned, move the artwork to the next portion; try to slide along the scanner's horizontal or vertical side rulers to maintain parallel lines on your different portions. You also need to make sure that you overlap the scanning areas (around 2–3cm/¾–1¼in) so that they can be easily matched later on.

4   Repeat step 3 until all your portions have been scanned. In Photoshop rotate the canvas of those portions facing the wrong way (Menu > Image > Rotate Canvas), then create a new document measuring the same size as your original artwork; in the resolution box type 300dpi, assuming that you have scanned your artwork at the same resolution.

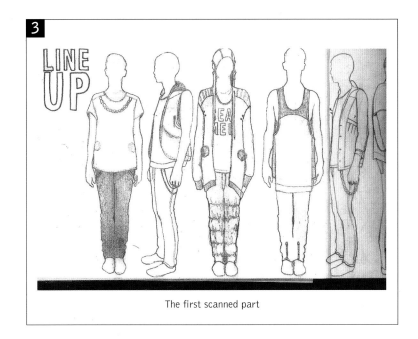

The first scanned part

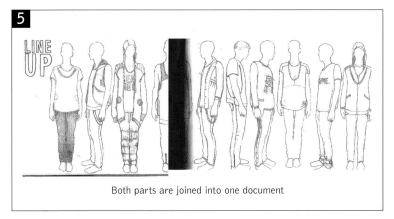

Both parts are joined into one document

5   In the Menu go to Window > your first scan file listed at the bottom (probably named Untitled-1). Then select your entire artwork: Menu > Select > All or (⌘ + A + or Ctrl + A for Windows PC) then copy it (⌘ + C or Ctrl + C for Windows PC) and paste it into your newly created file. Repeat the operation for all the different parts.

6

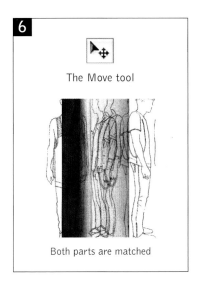

The Move tool

Both parts are matched

7

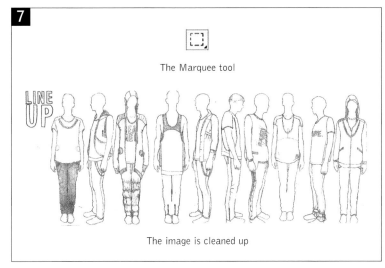

The Marquee tool

The image is cleaned up

8

The Layers pop-down menu is found on the top right of the window

The Crop tool

6 Use the Move tool to drag the different parts and align them as accurately as possible. You can also use the keyboard's arrow keys to nudge each part more precisely. Select the part that is on top by clicking on its icon in the Layers palette, then select Multiply in the Blending mode pop-down menu; this will make the white paper transparent, enabling you to see through the drawing and match precisely the overlapping parts.

7 When the two parts are matched correctly, in the overlapping area, look at which part can be deleted. Using the Marquee tool, select the unwanted area then press Delete. Finish by reverting Blending mode to Normal. Use the Eraser tool or the Lasso tool to clean up any remaining darkened areas.

8 Flatten the image by opening the Layers palette's menu and selecting Flatten Image. If necessary, use the Crop tool to frame the image better. The artwork can now be retouched.

9 As in the previous tutorial, use the Levels function to adjust the white and black balance of your illustration. With the Eraser tool clean off any remaining unwanted marks and stains.

10 If your illustration still looks a bit washed out after working on the Levels, you can remedy this by using the Curves function found in Menu > Image > Adjustments > Curves (⌘ + M + or Ctrl + M for Windows PC). At this early stage in the book, this is only a simple curve operation, so select in the Preset pop-up menu Darker (CS3 function only). Finish the artwork by doing a final clean up and retouch.

10

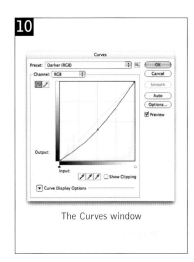

The Curves window

■ Quick tip

To make sure your illustration has the right greyscale level and that the white is really white, print your illustration. It is much easier and more accurate to verify this on paper; you can also spot any remaining stains and blemishes, which might have been overlooked on screen.

Neil Young, Final Line Up.

Howard Tangye,
Katya in Comme des Garçons;
Following the Line.
Pencils and oil on paper, Photoshop

Tutorial 3

Retouching and cleaning up illustrations imported from a digital camera

Drawing a fashion illustration on large formats is very rewarding and gives more room for expression, enabling natural media, such as charcoal or crayons, to be fully appreciated. When working on sizes such as A1 or even A0, scanning can become unwieldy; using a digital camera is the best way to digitize large-format illustration. Remember that taking a good-quality picture will save you lots of post-production time. It is also worth noting that today a digital camera's ubiquity makes it an easy choice for digitizing artwork at any size. Knowing how to work with a camera and understanding its inherent issues will help you take a better picture.

1   If you can afford it, use a good-quality SLR camera and a tripod to photograph your artwork. Natural daylight with no direct sunlight is always preferable for a good colour warmth and balance. Try to avoid using the flash since this often results in over-exposed areas.

2   In Photoshop, start by resizing the image; in this case we want an image size suitable for press printing, i.e. 300dpi and around 25cm (10in) in height. Digital images are usually 72 (on lower megapixel models) or 150dpi and are oversized compared to regular paper sizes.

3   Go to Menu > Image > Image Size or (⌘ + Alt + I or Ctrl + Alt + I for Windows PC) in the dialog window, enter 300dpi but before doing this make sure you un-tick Resample Image. Even if the size indicated in the Width and Height is still too big to fit your output size; press OK.

4   As in previous tutorials, use the Levels function to adjust the image's colour levels. As a further tip, once in the Levels window, select the black Eyedropper and hover around what looks like the

The original digital picture

The Image Size window

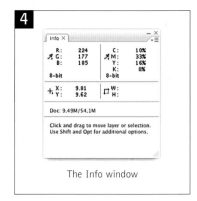

The Info window

darkest point – to help you better ascertain this use the Info palette (Menu > Window > Info), which gives you RGB values in real time (values closer to 0 are lightest and closer to 255 are darkest). Repeat with the white Eyedropper for the lightest point. Use the Curves function to boost the image's contrast since quite often digital snapshots are faded.

5   After correcting the Levels and the Curves, the image looks darker on the top; this is due to the way in which the photo was taken. Duplicate the layer (Menu > Layer > Duplicate Layer). With the Lasso tool select around the dark area of the image, and then create a new mask (icon at bottom of Layer palette). Now click on the icon with your illustration in the Layer palette next to the layer mask, and then select Curves (⌘ + M + or Ctrl + M for Windows PC). To adjust, use a preset such as Lighter; this will only affects the dark area, thanks to the mask.

6 Quite often, images taken with a digital camera are skewed. If so, use the Transform function to make the image straight again: Menu > Edit > Transform > Skew, then press and drag the corners of the bounding box so that the canvas on the picture is straight again.

7 The paper background is not textured enough and too uneven to retain, so it's better to knock it out and replace with a pure white background. Select the Magic Wand tool. In the Options bar set it to a tolerance of 32 with Anti-alias and Contiguous ticked. Click on the paper area once, then hold the Shift key and click again into a new area of paper, which has not yet been selected. Continue until the whole paper area is selected.

8 If there is a selection overspill into your illustration, try to input a lower tolerance in the Magic Wand Options bar. You can also lasso overspills away using the Alt key, while lassoing to subtract from the selection. When ready, go to Menu > Select > Inverse (↑ + ⌘ + I Mac or ↑ + Ctrl + I for Windows PC).

9 Follow by Menu > Select > Refine Edges (CS 3 Only, CS2 and previous version go to step 10) (Alt + ⌘ + R Mac or Alt + Ctrl + R for Windows PC). Select the preview icon, which gives you a white background, and play with the sliders to get a nice cutout of your illustration.

10 Finish by copy pasting the cutout illustration on a new layer. Create a new layer by clicking on the new layer icon at the bottom of the Layer palette, and then drag the new layer below the illustration and fill it with white: Menu > Edit > Fill.

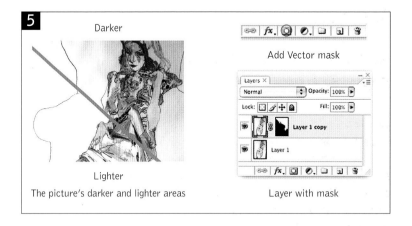

Darker

Lighter

The picture's darker and lighter areas

Add Vector mask

Layer with mask

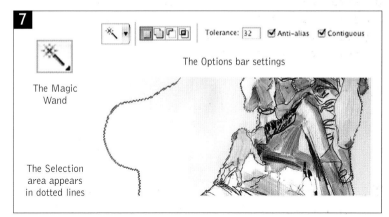

The Magic Wand

The Selection area appears in dotted lines

The Options bar settings

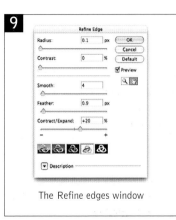

The Refine edges window

The New Layer icon

Howard Tangye,
Mya in John Galliano,
Paris Studio.
Pencils and oil on paper,
Photoshop

Howard Tangye,
George in Comme des Garçons,
Following the Line.
Pencils and oil on paper, Photoshop

Fiona Sinha,
Untitled.
Pencils, Photoshop

Hannah Morrison,
Mona.
Pencil, chalk, ink, Photoshop

Tutorial 4

Advanced retouching on scanned illustrations

Some scanned artwork requires more than just a few eraser strokes to get rid of blemishes, especially when paper textures or paint strokes are present. The illustration by Maria Teninzhiyan featured here has been created on two different papers with varying textures. To retouch this kind of work, I have used the Clone Stamp and the Healing Brush tool extensively. As this tutorial is very specific, I have used the first person throughout the tutorial; just adapt the skills to your own illustration.

1   The first step, as in previous tutorials, is to adjust the scanned image by modifying the Levels. I have also applied a Linear Contrast preset in the Curves window. On first observation, there is a vertical paper cut on the right with two different paper textures and this is where most of the work will take place.

2   Starting with the easy part, I select the Healing Brush tool and locate a small spot or stain, close to it but not too close. I press Alt + Click to select the sampling area, moving towards the stain, and single click over it. I move to the next stain and repeat the step. Note that you can right click to select a different brush diameter to suit the size of your spot or stain.

3   The cut line on the right requires several operations using different cloning techniques. I select the Clone Stamp tool and work it like the Healing Brush, making sure I avoid press and drag when cloning, which will smudge the artwork and make cloned areas obvious to spot. For this illustration I started with the clear-cut gap on the hem of the coat, which is easy to clone over. Remember to use quite small brush sizes when cloning.

4   The cut line above and below the silhouette where the background stands needs to be cleaned up. Since it is a straight line I drag a guide line from the vertical ruler then, using the Rectangular Marquee tool, I select an area flush with the edge of the cut line and around 2cm (¾in) to the left of it. This area will be the frame in which the cloning operation takes place. I then clone away the dark line, avoiding any spill-over thanks to the selection area.

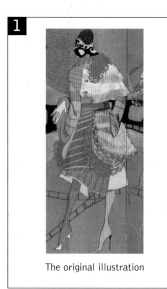

1

The original illustration

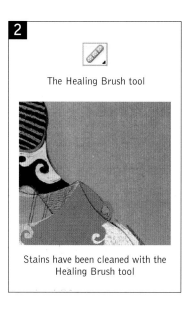

2

The Healing Brush tool

Stains have been cleaned with the Healing Brush tool

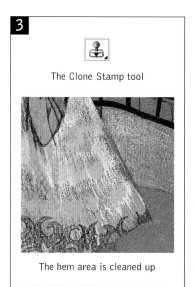

3

The Clone Stamp tool

The hem area is cleaned up

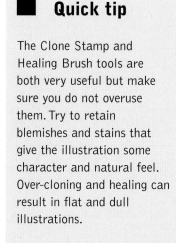

■ **Quick tip**

The Clone Stamp and Healing Brush tools are both very useful but make sure you do not overuse them. Try to retain blemishes and stains that give the illustration some character and natural feel. Over-cloning and healing can result in flat and dull illustrations.

4

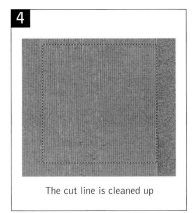

The cut line is cleaned up

5

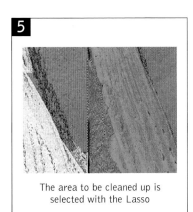

The area to be cleaned up is
selected with the Lasso

6

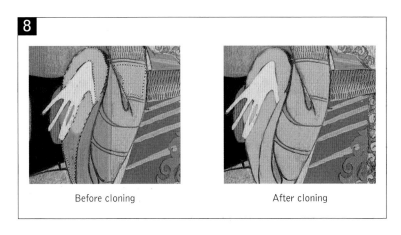

Before cleaning up   After cleaning up

5 Some areas along the line have elements painted on top of the background colour so using the Rectangular Marquee tool does not work well, instead I use the Lasso tool and select along the vertical guide and around the background, avoiding any other painted areas.

6 The next cloning operation involves getting rid of a large area, such as the one on the middle right edge, a remnant part of a silhouette, which was cropped away. I start by lassoing around the unwanted area. Just above this area is a nice clean background, so I move the lasso selection onto the background area. Next, I copy and paste the background then use the Move tool to move the pasted selection on top of the area to hide.

7 I finish the operation by retouching the edges and inside the pasted patch to discard any easily spotted repeat between the patch and the background above it. To clone between layers, I select Sample: Current & Below in the Clone Stamp tool options bar settings. I repeat the operation for any other similar areas.

7

The Options bar settings

8 The last cloning operation is on the right arm, which has a colour and texture change. There is no big enough area to cover the arm in one go as in the previous step. First I lasso around the area that needs to change and then I sample from a small area on the right, making sure I do not go beyond the clean area of my cloning source.

9 I finish the retouching by printing out the artwork to check on paper any mistakes or remaining stains. Make sure you always keep and save your artwork in Photoshop format with all the layers retained so you can at any time retouch or alter your artwork.

8

Before cloning   After cloning

Maria Teninzhiyan,
Bon Voyage.
Gouache, pastels and Photoshop

Peir Wu,
Jarvis.
Ink, watercolour, Photoshop

30.

Adam Rogers,
Final Collection design
developments.
Mixed media, Photoshop

Katinka Saltzmann,
Der Gedanke.
Waterproof ink, aquarelle,
Photoshop

Chapter 2
Colouring illustrations

This second chapter looks specifically at how to add colours on to scanned illustrations and constitutes the first easy steps towards digital painting.

Applying solid colour to a scanned hand-drawn illustration with a computer is the digital equivalent of filling in colours with marker pens or pencils. There are many advantages to colouring an illustration digitally over natural media: speed, cost and edition to name but a few. Time taken to fill in colours on a scanned illustration can be a fraction of what it is when done manually. This chapter

contains artwork using mainly flat, solid colours and some pattern fill colours, which is the easiest and most basic way to colour in a drawing in Photoshop. Solid colour blocking with the Paint Bucket tool or the Fill function is great for delivering fast visualization on any scanned artwork.

The methodology for digitally colouring illustrations in Photoshop starts with the specific preparation of the artwork after scanning, followed by the filling in of each colour, finishing with how to easily replace colours.

Tutorial highlights

Tutorial 1
The first tutorial helps you understand the basics of digital colouring, how to prepare the illustration and how to perform simple solid colour fills.

Tutorial 2
The second tutorial deals with simple digital painting and how to get the best out of the Paintbrush tool. Also included are gradients and adjustment layers.

Key skills:	Application:	Key tools:	Key menu functions:
Digital colouring	Photoshop	Brush tool	Menu > Edit > Fill
Basic painting		Paint Bucket tool	Menu > Window > Brushes
Working with layers		Lasso tool	Menu > Select > Inverse
Gradients			Menu > Image > Adjustments > Hue/Saturation
Colour and area selection			

Inke Ehmsen,
Lost Garden.
Pencil, Illustrator, Photoshop

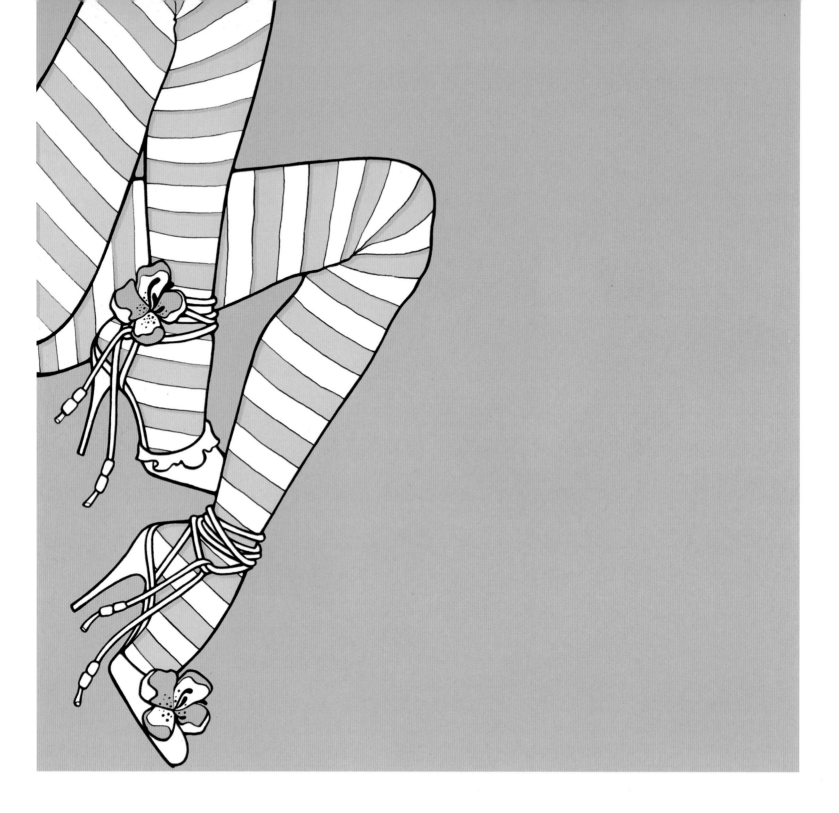

Natalie Ferstendik,
Pin-up, *Sunday Times Style Magazine.*
Dip pen, ink, Photoshop

Natalie Ferstendik,
Pearl, *Sunday Times Style Magazine.*
Dip pen, ink, Photoshop

Tutorial 1

Basic digital colouring

Moving on from the first chapter where illustrations were only retouched and mainly created outside the computer, digital colouring on a black-and-white hand-drawn illustration stands halfway between natural and digital media. Below are the basic steps needed to produce digital colouring.

1 Start by scanning your artwork and cleaning it up as explained in Chapter 1. Before you can apply colour into different parts of your scanned artwork, you need closed 'watertight' areas delimited by unbroken lines. If any given area has a gap in the artwork line, the colour will leak out into the adjacent area. Look closely at your illustration to spot any gaps, that need to be closed.

2 Set your View to Actual Pixels, scroll around the artwork towards an area where you spotted a gap between two lines, using the Hand tool. To work faster, you can hold the space bar while pressing and dragging your mouse; this automatically selects the Hand tool.

3 Select the Eyedropper tool and, with it, point towards a drawn line close to a gap. Single click to clone and select the colour of the drawn line. This will update the foreground colour in the Tools palette, making sure that when filling the gap the same colour is used.

4 First select the Brush tool, then select a style and size of brush matching your original artwork line by right clicking anywhere on the artwork window or Menu > Window > Brushes. For the pictured artwork, a soft round brush with a diameter of 3 pixels was selected.

5 Press and drag the mouse to create a brush stroke closing the gap; try to give the stroke a smooth and realistic look. If you have a graphics tablet, this is where it comes in handy. Repeat the same action on all gaps to be closed on your artwork.

6 In the Tools palette, select the Magic Wand tool, then point and click onto an area to be coloured in. If more than one delimited area needs to be filled in with the same colour, select it by clicking on it while pressing the Shift key. If you have selected an area by mistake press Alt and click on it again to deselect it.

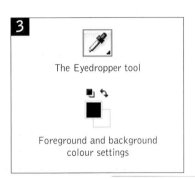

The original scanned image

Gaps in the illustration

The Hand tool

The Eyedropper tool

Foreground and background colour settings

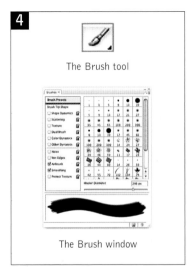

The Brush tool

The Brush window

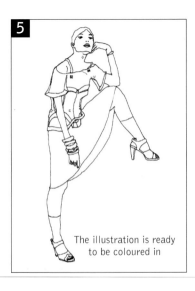

The illustration is ready to be coloured in

7 In the Layer palette click on the new layer icon or select New Layer in the palette pop-up menu. Next, point and click on the foreground colour swatch in the Tools palette, and in the Colour Picker window select a suitable colour (in this case a skin tone).

8 Select the Paint Bucket tool, point and click onto any one of the selected areas to fill it in. Or without selecting the Paint Bucket tool, go to: Menu > Edit > Fill. Using the Fill function rather than the Paint Bucket lets you choose a colour at the same time, thus saving time in the process.

9 Select the Background layer by clicking on to it in the Layer palette, then repeat steps 6 to 8 for each new colour to apply onto your artwork. Make sure every new colour has its own layer.

■ **Quick tip**

To get a slicker and crisper illustration with a pure black outline, scan your illustration in Line art mode at 1200dpi or after cleaning up a regular 300dpi colour mode scanned drawing go to Menu > Image > Mode > Greyscale, then Menu > Image > Mode > Bitmap. In the Bitmap window choose 1200dpi and 50% Threshold. Finish by converting back your illustration to RGB image mode and resizing the image to the original size (300dpi).

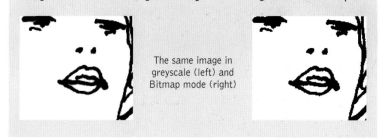

The same image in greyscale (left) and Bitmap mode (right)

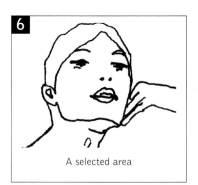

6 A selected area

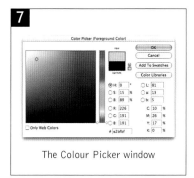

7 The Colour Picker window

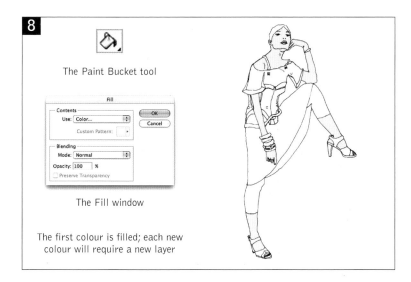

8

The Paint Bucket tool

The Fill window

The first colour is filled; each new colour will require a new layer

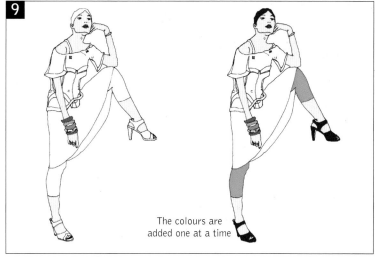

9

The colours are added one at a time

10 To change any given colour on your illustration, single click the layer on which you want to make the change then press ⌘ (or ctrl for Windows PC), while single clicking on the layer's thumbnail to select the layer's content. Create a new layer, then go to: Menu > Edit > Fill and choose a new colour. Finish by Hiding or discarding the layer containing the previous colour. You can easily create colour variations by Saving As several version of your illustration.

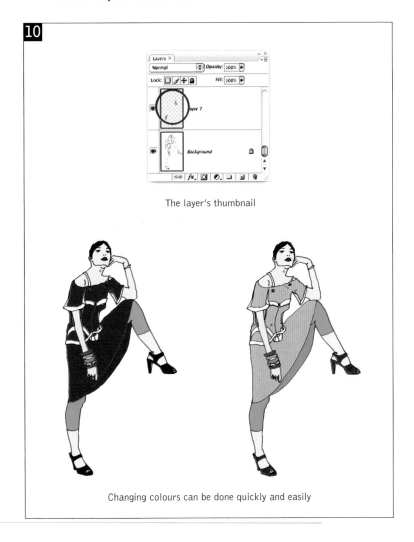

The layer's thumbnail

Changing colours can be done quickly and easily

Binia Umland, Untitled.

Nathalie Hughes,
Baby Doll.
Fine-point ink pen, ArcSoft
PhotoStudio

Avigail Claire,
Triangles, bear and circle.
Pen, Photoshop

Avigail Claire,
Pom-pom.
Black ink pen, Photoshop

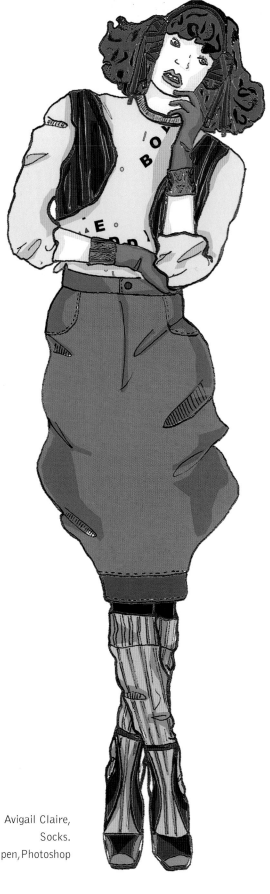

Avigail Claire,
Socks.
Black ink pen, Photoshop

All of Danny's drawings are done
with black fine-tip pens. Once the
outline is finished, they are scanned
in. When developing colour
illustrations, Danny mixes natural
media such as watercolour and
digital colouring in Photoshop: 'I try
to blend real materials with digital
to make it hard to tell which is
which. Different paper textures help
achieve this effect but also
compositing within different layers.'
Danny Roberts

Danny Roberts,
The Girl in the Red Dress.
Black felt-tip pen, Photoshop

Danny Roberts,
Gypsy Girl.
Black felt-tip pen, Photoshop

Danny Roberts,
Waiting Room.
Black felt-tip pen, Photoshop

Tutorial 2

Basic digital painting

There are many different ways to add colour onto a scanned illustration; the previous tutorial dealt only with basic colour fills. Digital painting is the main technique to simulate natural media and tools such as paintbrushes and marker pens commonly found in a fashion illustrator's toolbox. This tutorial only deals with basic digital painting and other fill techniques such as gradients; for further tutorials on this subject go to Chapter 7. Working with digital 'natural media' offers the advantage of not having to make the drawing's black outlines 'watertight' as in the previous tutorial. Illustrations coloured in with the Paintbrush tool look much more natural, like a fashion sketch.

This tutorial has been divided into three mini-tutorials, each dealing with different digital colouring techniques.

Creating gradients

Photoshop excels at making custom gradients, here is how:

1 Once your scanned black-and-white drawing is ready to be coloured in, go to Menu > Select > Color Range; in the Select pop-up menu choose Highlights. Then Menu > Select > Inverse (or ⌘ + ↑ + I or Ctrl + ↑ + I for Windows PC). Next copy paste your selection (⌘ + C then ⌘ + V or Ctrl + C then Ctrl + V for Windows PC). You have created a new layer containing only the drawing without the white background.

2 Create another new layer and drag it below the layer with your illustration and above the Background layer. Select the Gradient tool; in the option bar select a gradient type and if desired a gradient preset. You can also design your own gradient by selecting a custom foreground and background colour in the Tool palette. Finish by pressing and dragging the Gradient tool across your artwork canvas. Experiment with different kinds of direction and length when dragging.

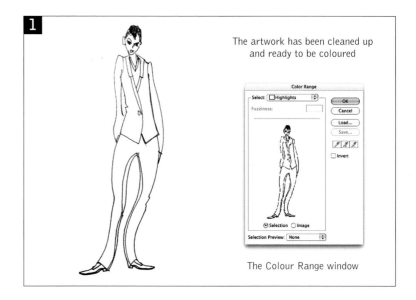

1

The artwork has been cleaned up and ready to be coloured

The Colour Range window

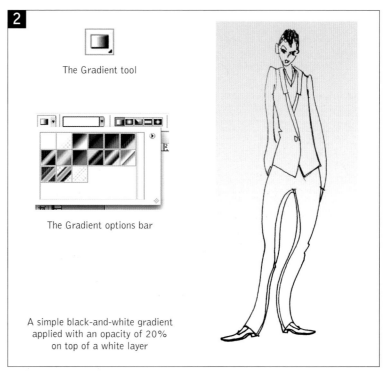

2

The Gradient tool

The Gradient options bar

A simple black-and-white gradient applied with an opacity of 20% on top of a white layer

Colouring with the Paintbrush

For a more natural media look and feel, such as paint or pencils, try Photoshop's Paintbrush tool, but do use a graphics tablet! Here is how to achieve simple solid or layered colouring with Photoshop's Paintbrush:

3 Start by creating a new layer (making sure it stands below your drawing's layer), then select the Brush tool and a colour to fill in. Right click anywhere on the art board to select a brush type and diameter. Click on the top-right pop-up menu to load other brush presets, such as for example Dry Media Brushes. Think of what kind of media you want to emulate digitally.

4 Each new colour should have a new layer. The Paintbrush opacity must be set at 100 per cent if you want a flat, solid look, while

The Opacity sets the colour's transparency; the Flow sets how much paint is applied as you brush over an area

for a more natural and realistic look, drop the opacity down. You will need to release the mouse button or lift your stylus for each stroke to apply additional colour on top of a previous stroke.

5 Toggle between the Brush and the Eraser to get rid of mistakes, making sure that the Eraser has the same Brush Preset as the Paintbrush. Use different brush sizes to give the illustration a more realistic look; thinner lines on edges and design details, wider ones for fills.

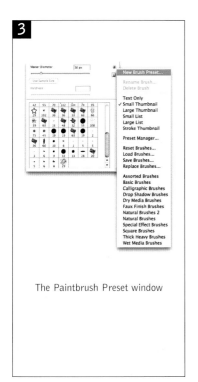

The Paintbrush Preset window

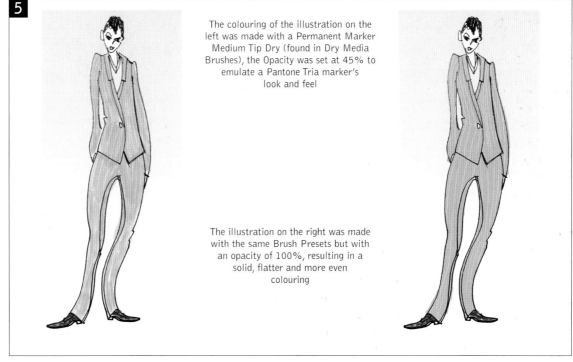

The colouring of the illustration on the left was made with a Permanent Marker Medium Tip Dry (found in Dry Media Brushes), the Opacity was set at 45% to emulate a Pantone Tria marker's look and feel

The illustration on the right was made with the same Brush Presets but with an opacity of 100%, resulting in a solid, flatter and more even colouring

Adjusting colours

Photoshop can easily adjust colours painted in any illustration and having created a layer per colour gives you even more control. There are countless ways to adjust colours. Here is a technique to swiftly alter your illustration's colours.

6 Select the layer on which you wish to alter the colour; duplicate it (drag the layer onto the new layer icon) to keep a safe version of the original colour, Hide the original layer (click on the eye icon). Go to Menu > Image > Adjustments > Hue/Saturation (or ⌘ + U or Ctrl + U for Windows PC). In the Hue/Saturation window, move the Hue slider to change the colour or hue; move the Saturation slider to saturate or de-saturate the colour. Use the Lightness slider to darken or lighten the colour.

7 If you want to alter the whole image or parts of it, create an adjustment layer as follows: in the Layer palette, click on the adjustment layer icon, select Hue/Saturation. In the Hue/Saturation window, press OK without changing anything. Drag the Adjustment layer up or down between the different colour layers. The Adjustment layer will only affect the layers placed below it. You can also move around the colour layers if you don't want them to be affected, but make sure this does not alter the look of your illustration. Double click on the adjustment layer icon to change the Hue/Saturation.

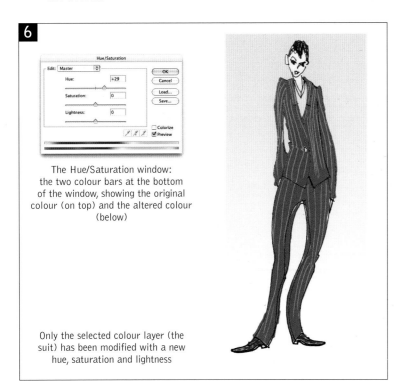

6

The Hue/Saturation window:
the two colour bars at the bottom
of the window, showing the original
colour (on top) and the altered colour
(below)

Only the selected colour layer (the
suit) has been modified with a new
hue, saturation and lightness

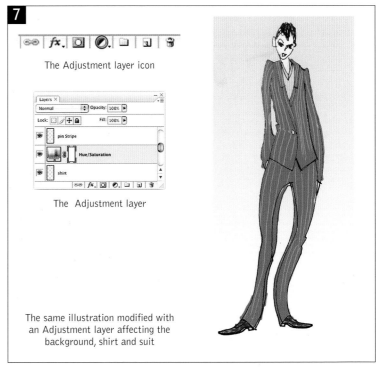

7

The Adjustment layer icon

The Adjustment layer

The same illustration modified with
an Adjustment layer affecting the
background, shirt and suit

This final illustration has had other Adjustment layers added, such as Channel Mixer and Colour Balance. Kevin Tallon, Untitled.

Kevin Tallon,
Denim Wonder.
Felt-tip pen, Photoshop

Shaun Samson,
Goldie.
Pen, Illustrator, Photoshop

Shaun Samson,
Camera Man.
Pen, Illustrator, Photoshop

William Kroll,
Country Life with Grouse.
Pen, Photoshop

William Kroll,
Country Life with Deer.
Pen, Photoshop

Chapter 3

Illustrations with textiles, patterns and textures

Adding texture, patterns and fabrics into an illustration can be achieved in various ways with Photoshop, and this chapter explains and showcases key techniques, tricks and tips on how to do this best.

Textiles and textures applied to a digital fashion illustration enable a better visual communication of a given design; it also constitutes the first step into 'compositing' work with various media: scans or pictures of fabric mixed with freehand drawings and digital painting.

Photoshop features a dedicated Texturizer filter and various pattern styles. The Texturizer filter can help build any kind of texture for a fabric or flat background either from scratch or from a scanned image with various controls to perfect the look and feel. The Pattern Maker can create repeat patterns on any given surface and from scratch or from any given file. Creativity and experimentation rules when pattern, textures and textiles are concerned.

Tutorial highlights

Tutorial 1
Starting nice and easy, this first tutorial explains the principles of working with scanned or web-sourced images of textiles and how to include them in an illustration with a simple copy paste operation. It also looks also into how to create custom patterns and shading using the Paintbrush tool.

Tutorial 2
The second tutorial covers more advanced and interactive techniques to manipulate fabrics and images once imported on to illustrations; including the Warp tool, Texturizer filter and Blending modes.

Key skills:	Application:	Key tools:	Key menu functions:
Adding fabrics to illustrations	Photoshop	Brush tool	Menu > Edit > Fill
Developing textures		Magic Wand	Menu > Filter > Textures > Texturizer
Applying patterns		Warp tool	Menu > Filter > Pattern Maker
Paste into			Menu > Image > Canvas Size
Noise reduction			Menu > Filter > Sharpen > Sharpen
Free transform			Menu > Filter > Noise > Reduce Noise
Layer blending modes			Menu > Edit > Paste Into
			Menu > Image > Canvas Size
			Menu > Layer > Flatten Image
			Menu > Edit > Define Pattern
			Menu > Edit > Free Transform
			Menu > Image > Adjustments > Channel Mixer
			Menu > Filter > Texture > Texturizer

Ploi Horwang,
Up Yours.
Pencil, Photoshop

Ploi Horwang,
I'm a Dog.
Pencil, Photoshop

'My illustrations are fun, inspired by funny poses and bold colours. Most of my work is based on quirky models in magazines or my friends posing for my digital camera. I start by drawing with pencil on paper and then I scan into Photoshop. I then edit my picture using the Level function to strengthen the contrast. I then add in colours and some shading to add depth. I like to experiment with Photoshop; sometimes this results in amazing colours and effects. I still prefer working with a pencil and paper to produce more natural illustrations before using the computer.' Ploi Horwang

Ploi Horwang,
Boomboxboy.
Pencil, Photoshop

Tutorial 1

Compositing: adding fabric and creating patterns

The illustration created for this tutorial by Pia Bleiht includes three distinctive elements: a scanned freehand illustration, a digitally composed background and scanned fabrics. The act of merging these elements into one composition is called compositing. Added to this and moving on from the previous tutorial, digital painting in the form of shading is added to bring the illustration alive.

1 Begin the compositing process by scanning in or downloading from the web the various necessary elements. Try to be aware of sizing: your illustration size and aspect ratio should be the same as other elements. A good trick is to quickly print out the various parts and mock them up on paper.

2 Clean up the illustration as explained in Chapter 1; resize any digital source images if necessary. If you need to enlarge a digital image sourced on the web, make sure you do as follows: go to Menu > Image > Image Size (or ⌘ + Alt + I or Ctrl + Alt + I for Windows PC). Tick Resample Image and select Bicubic

Smoother (CS2 or CS3, select Bicubic if not), enter values for the Document Size and Resolution. Make sure that the difference between the old and new pixel dimension (at the top of window) is not too big, as this will result in pixelated images.

3 If you need to enlarge your web-sourced image quite a bit to match your scanned illustration, try to soften the pixelation by using: Menu > Filter > Sharpen > Sharpen. You can also try Menu > Filter > Noise > Reduce Noise. To reduce the noise most, Preserve Details and Sharpen Details sliders should have a low percentage. Be careful not to overdo it or your image will become blurry.

4 Next, as in Chapter 2's first tutorial, the skin colour is applied; since the illustration style is neat and all the lines are 'watertight', a simple Magic Wand tool selection of each area to colour will suffice. Do not forget to create a new layer. Fill the colour in with the Fill function.

5 Create a new layer and select a colour and brush suitable for producing shading (in this case a 17px soft-edge brush with low opacity and flow). Tick on the Airbrush icon; this emulates a

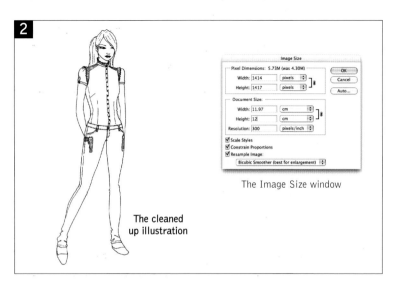

The Image Size window

The cleaned
up illustration

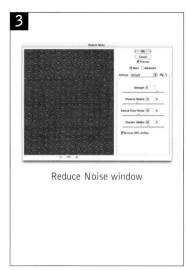

Reduce Noise window

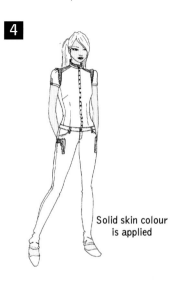

Solid skin colour
is applied

5

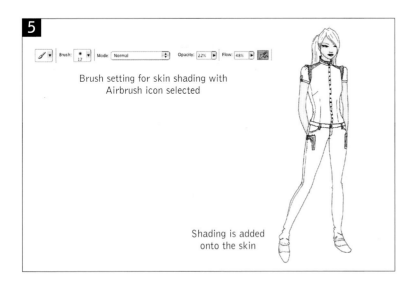

Brush setting for skin shading with
Airbrush icon selected

Shading is added
onto the skin

6

The denim fabric file

7

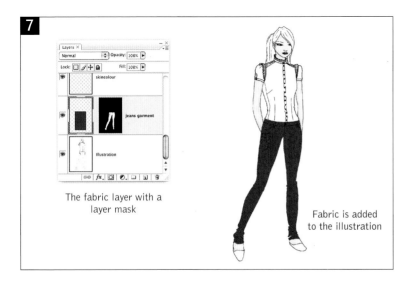

The fabric layer with a
layer mask

Fabric is added
to the illustration

classic airbrush feel that is great for creating shading. Build up your shading starting, from the outer edge, working inwards. If you get into difficulty use the History window to step back.

6 Fabric will now be added to the illustration. Start by opening your fabric scan or web image. Again, make sure that the fabric image size will easily fit into the area it is intended for. Select All (⌘ + A or Ctrl + A for Windows PC) and Copy (⌘ + C or Ctrl + C for Windows PC). Switch back to the illustration file.

7 With the Magic Wand and in the illustration layer select the area to fill in with fabric then go to Menu > Edit > Paste Into (or ↑ + ⌘ + V or ↑ + Ctrl + V for Windows PC). Note how Photoshop has created a new layer with a mask around the selected area to fill.

8 The fabric for the top is created in the same way as the denim but needs a pattern to simulate a print repeat. To create a simple pattern with step, start by sourcing an image with a single element to repeat (it must have a white background). Open it in Photoshop, make the canvas size twice as big: Menu > Image > Canvas Size (or ⌘ + Alt +C or Ctrl + Alt + C for Windows PC). Copy paste and drag the element towards the bottom right; flatten the image: Menu > Layer > Flatten Image. Finish by cropping the image as close a possible to both elements. To create the pattern go to Menu > Edit > Define Pattern, give it a name.

8

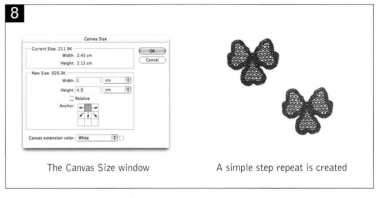

The Canvas Size window   A simple step repeat is created

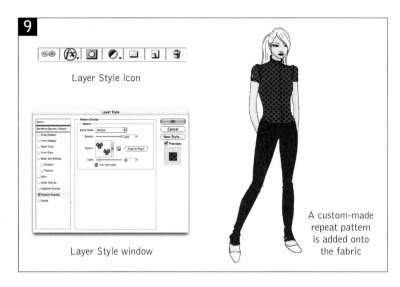

Layer Style icon

Layer Style window

A custom-made
repeat pattern
is added onto
the fabric

9 Switch to the illustration file; select the layer with the top fabric.
Click on the Add a Layer Style icon; select Pattern Overlay. In
the window choose the newly created pattern, give it the right
scale and select Multiply in the Blending mode pop up menu.

10 The illustration was finished off with more digital painting over
the garments, face and hair. The background was composed in
Illustrator then imported into Photoshop (see Chapter 6). The
flat drawings were developed in Illustrator.

■ Quick tip

Sometimes a fabric sample is not big enough or satisfactory. From
a small swatch, you can create a bigger one as follows: make the
fabric's document canvas size the same size as the garment to be
filled in. With the Rectangle Marquee tool select within the fabric
swatch an area that has no obvious markings (creases or marks).
Copy paste it enough times to cover the area to fill in, flatten the
image and use the Clone Stamp tool to erase the obvious tiling
marks. The denim in this tutorial was created in such a way.

Pia Bleiht Kristianson,
Baby's on Fire.

Natalie Hughes,
Girl in Prada Headband.
Fine ink pens, ArcSoft PhotoStudio

Inke Ehmsen,
Lost Time.
Pencil, Illustrator, Photoshop

Mia Overgaard,
Featherboy.
Pencil, Photoshop

Mia Overgaard,
88. Jacket and dress by Lanvin.
Photoshop

Avigail Claire,
All over print.
Black ink pen, Photoshop

Avigail Claire,
The bear and the leopard.
Black ink pen, Photoshop

Tutorial 2

Compositing:
manipulating fabric and creating textures

Moving on from this chapter's first tutorial, here are a few more advanced techniques to compose an illustration with fabric, texture and scanned artwork. The main difference is in the manipulation of imported fabrics using the Free Transform and Warp tools, which enable the fine-tuning of any placed fabric's look and feel, for example, the fabric's grain line and proportions. The other area of this tutorial is Blending modes and the use of web or library pictures as elements of an illustration.

1 As in the previous tutorial, source all the components of your composition, scan and clean up the drawn illustration, and check all aspect ratios and document sizes before starting the compositing work in Photoshop. For this tutorial the composition contains scanned, web-sourced fabrics and several web pictures for other elements.

2 We will start with adding the trouser fabric. Use the same methodology as in the previous tutorial (Copy, Paste Into), but this time only select one leg. If you cannot do this because both legs are not separate 'watertight' entities, select them both with the Magic Wand and then subtract (pressing Alt while you do this) from your selection using the Polygonal Lasso tool.

3 Once both legs have fabric pasted into them, select the layer of either one of them, go to Menu > Edit > Free Transform (or ⌘ + T or Ctrl + T for Windows PC). Rotate the fabric to match the grain line using the Free Transform bounding box by pressing and dragging on one of its corners (to do this, you might need to zoom out to view the entire bounding box).

4 Next comes the jacket. For this, a plaid fabric sourced from the web has been manipulated using the Channel Mixer

The scanned
and cleaned-up illustration

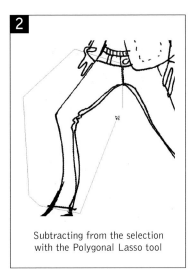

Subtracting from the selection
with the Polygonal Lasso tool

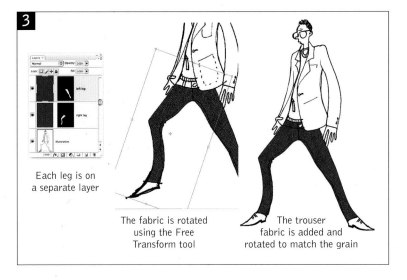

Each leg is on
a separate layer

The fabric is rotated
using the Free
Transform tool

The trouser
fabric is added and
rotated to match the grain

(Menu > Image > Adjustments > Channel Mixer). The fabric was also repeated and seamlessly matched from a small sample. All the various parts of the jacket are filled in with plaid fabric and rotated to fit the grain. You can also move the plaid to align it, by pressing and dragging inside the Transform bounding box.

4

The small original web sourced
fabric sample

The same fabric seamlessly repeated
and coloured

The plaid fabric is added to the jacket

6

Dragging a selection
across two documents

7

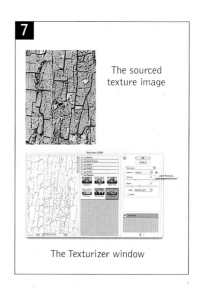

The sourced
texture image

The Texturizer window

5

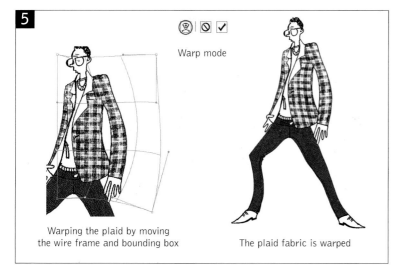

Warp mode

Warping the plaid by moving
the wire frame and bounding box

The plaid fabric is warped

5 To produce a more realistic look on the jacket, rotating the fabric is not enough, so the Warp mode is used as follows: select the fabric layer to be warped (in this case, the left arm), press ⌘ + T (or Ctrl + T for Windows PC). Click on the Warp tool symbol in the Options bar; press and drag the wire frame to create a curvature on the fabric matching the illustration.

6 A fun way to compose in Photoshop is to use and include specific elements of sourced images in a fashion illustration. Here an old mirror picture is to be used for the aviator sunglasses. Start by selecting one of the sunglasses lens area with the Magic Wand, or Lasso tool if the area is not a closed shape. Open the sourced image; arrange both document windows to sit next to each other on your screen. Select the Rectangular Marquee tool, press and drag the selection on your illustration across to the sourced image file. Move the selection to best fit the image, copy the selection and paste it back in the illustration file.

7 Customized textures can easily be created in Photoshop. For this tutorial a cracked leather look is sought for the shoes, here is how: source an image with an interesting texture, and save it as a Photoshop file. Create a new document measuring the same size as your illustration (including DPI size). Go to Menu > Filter > Texture > Texturizer, click on the Load Texture button and open your source image file. Move the Scaling and Relief sliders to get the desired texture look and feel. Press OK to confirm.

Texture is added on the shoes

New layer with solid colour fill

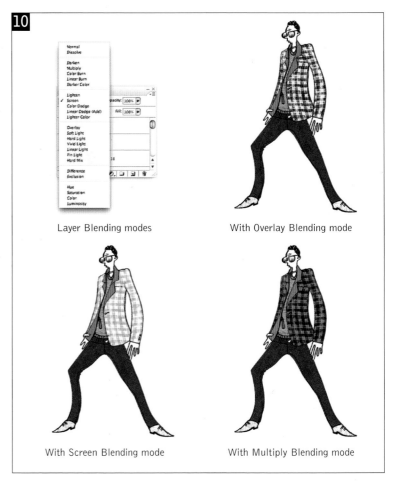

Layer Blending modes

With Overlay Blending mode

With Screen Blending mode

With Multiply Blending mode

8 Still in the new document file, Select All and Copy. (⌘ + A then ⌘ + C or Ctrl + A then Ctrl + C for Windows PC). Switch to your illustration file, select the area to be 'texturized' with the Wand or Lasso. Then Paste Into (↑ + ⌘ + V or ↑ + Ctrl + V for Windows PC). Just as with the fabric of the jacket, you can Free Transform (rotate, scale, warp, etc.) the pasted texture to get your desired look.

9 With Layer Blending modes, the fabric colour, look and feel can be quickly altered as follows: select an area with a fabric on your illustration layer (i.e. the jacket). Create a new layer, fill the layer with colour and make sure the layer is above the various fabric layers.

10 Next, in the Layer window and with the new colour filled layer selected, press on the Blending mode pop-up menu (Normal button) and select a Blending mode. You can experiment with different Blending modes to find a desired look.

■ Quick tip

Blending mode is a major area for compositing and painting in Photoshop. Think of Blending modes as an interaction between two layers (or between a painted and background colour). The interaction will differ depending on which Blending mode is selected. Results vary widely depending on the blend colour and the base colour.

Kevin Tallon,
Crack Shoes.

Eugene Lin,
Saving Ferragamo, Look 04.
Pens, Photoshop and scanned
fabrics

Eugene Lin,
Saving Ferragamo, Look 05.
Pens, Photoshop and scanned
fabrics

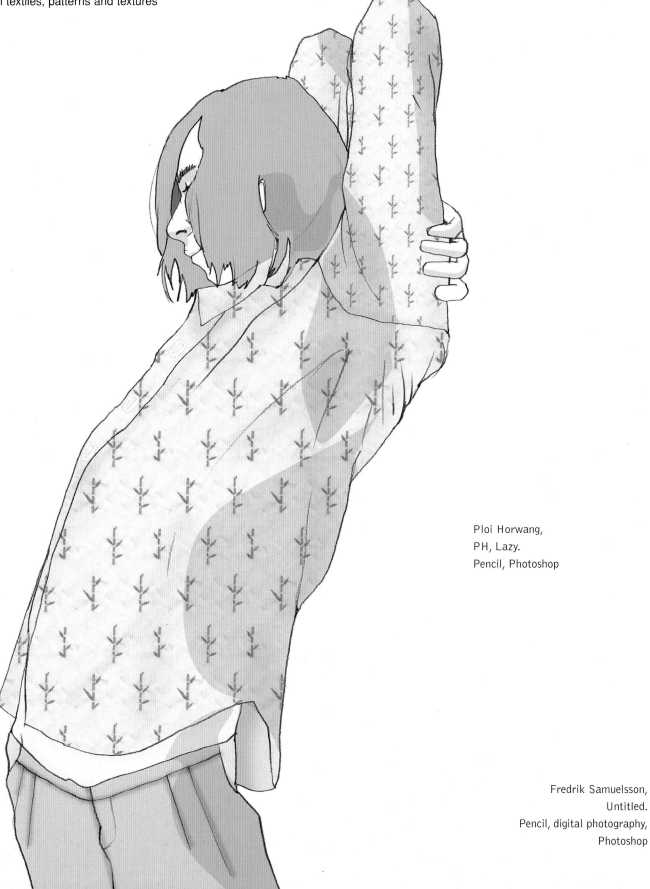

Ploi Horwang,
PH, Lazy.
Pencil, Photoshop

Fredrik Samuelsson,
Untitled.
Pencil, digital photography,
Photoshop

Chapter 4
Vector illustrations

Fashion illustrations created with vector applications, such as Adobe Illustrator, have an instantly recognizable visual identity. Originally created in the early to mid 1990s, this genre has remained to the fore of fashion illustration trends by constantly evolving and adapting to visual preferences and tastes.

The slick and solid-coloured look delivered by vector graphics has been the technological driving force behind the creative experimentation and output of vector illustrations. In the early 1990s, being able to easily solid fill any surface at the click of the mouse was radical, inspiring countless illustrators such as Jason Brooks, whose seminal illustrations defined the genre. Today's developments in vector applications mean that more and more is possible and that the boundaries between Adobe Photoshop and Illustrator that were previously so clear are harder to define today. The kinds of vector illustrations featured in this chapter are usually either developed by tracing a scanned freehand sketch or a picture. Working with a template is a logical transition step from developing illustrations mainly by hand to working solely on the computer. Tracing with Illustrator is also easier than painting on Photoshop, thus starting with vector illustration enables a gentler learning curve.

Tutorial highlights

Tutorial 1
The first tutorial focuses on the basics of vector tracing, using the Pencil tool and working with a template image. Highlights will feature how to colour fill and use pictures as colour fills.

Tutorial 2
The second tutorial features more advanced and subtle vector graphics-tracing techniques with the Pen tool; also featured are Adobe Illustrator's Symbols.

Key skills:

Tracing from drawings or
    pictures
Creating vector illustrations
Colour fill
Applying images to vector
    objects
Symbols
Outline stroke
Object expand
Creating pattern swatches

Application:

Illustrator

Key tools:

Pen tool
Pencil tool
Smooth tool
Symbol Sprayer tool

Key menu functions:

Menu > Window > Swatch Libraries > Colour Books
Menu > Window > Brush Libraries > Artistic
Menu > Window > Pathfinder
Menu > Object > Path > Outline Stroke
Menu > Window > Symbol Libraries
Menu > Object > Expand

Maria Cardelli,
The Flower Hat.
Illustrator

Maria Cardelli,
Lying in the garden.
Illustrator

Maria Cardelli,
Lulu's lingerie.
Illustrator

Tutorial 1:

Vector tracing with the Pencil tool

Vector graphics are made up of segments (lines) and anchor points, which are either regular (for straight segments) or with Bezier curves (for curved segments). The main tools used to create vector graphics are the Pen, Pencil and Brush. This first tutorial focuses on the Pencil tool, which is easier to work with than the Pen tool. When drawing with the Pencil tool, anchor points and segments are laid onto the art board. Illustrator automatically decides where anchor points and segments are best positioned. A vector object usually has a Fill colour and a Stroke (outline) colour. For this tutorial, I strongly recommend using a graphics tablet for better accuracy and faster workflow, but most importantly it makes the Pencil tool drawing experience so much better.

1 Start by selecting a picture you want to trace, making sure if it is from the web that it is not too small – usually around 100kB is fine. Open the picture in Illustrator. In the Layer palette (Menu > Window > Layers), click on the Lock Layer box (next to the Eye icon) to lock the layer. This will facilitate the tracing, avoiding the image from moving around.

2 Create a new layer and select the Pencil tool in the Tool palette. To facilitate the tracing process, select a colour for the Stroke (double click on the Stroke icon), which is not on the picture (usually a bright pink or green does the job), then select No Colour for the Fill (click on the No Fill icon).

3 For each colour you will need to trace a different object; think about how you want your illustration to look and which colours should go where. To begin the tracing, press and drag the Pencil tool above the template image where you want to start an object, go around it smoothly and come back to your starting point. Make sure you overlap the tracing slightly at the start/finish point to avoid any gaps when you colour fill the shape later on and to virtually close the shape.

4 Move on to the next object to trace. Think about which object is in front of which; you should start by drawing the objects placed at the back and finish with the ones in front. If objects

1

The template picture is open in Illustrator

The layer is locked

2

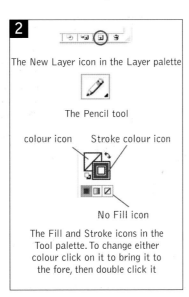

The New Layer icon in the Layer palette

The Pencil tool

colour icon   Stroke colour icon

No Fill icon

The Fill and Stroke icons in the Tool palette. To change either colour click on it to bring it to the fore, then double click it

3

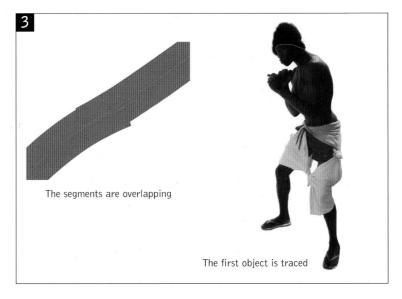

The segments are overlapping

The first object is traced

Quick tip

When working with the Pencil tool, it is important to set the tool option to suit your drawing style. Double click on the Pencil tool icon to access the tool's preference window. Fidelity controls the distance between anchor points – the higher the value, the fewer anchor points within a drawn path. Smoothness regulates how much a drawn line is smoothed – the higher the value, the smoother the path. Edit Selected Path, when ticked, enables you to merge the previous drawn path with a new one as long as you start it within the set pixel range. This is very useful for drawing long paths in small yet connected sections.

The Pencil tool preferences window

are on top of each other, draw the one behind first. To avoid gaps, always draw a complete outline even if there is a shape above cutting into it. In this case the whole outline of the body is drawn first, then the arms and the facial details.

5 Carry on with the other major elements of the illustration using the Pencil tool. If you are not happy with a shape's curve, which contains bumps or kinks, try using the Smooth tool. Simply select the traced object with the black arrow and with the Smooth tool retrace the curves over a bump – this should smooth it out.

6 Try to develop a style when tracing; you do not need to trace the template image accurately and you can streamline the smaller details away. Don't hesitate to draw several versions on different layers with different tracing styles to get a good feel for the Pencil tool and working with a graphics tablet.

7 Illustrator handles many different colour libraries such as Pantone. You can access them in: Menu > Window > Swatch Libraries > Colour Books (CS3 only) > Pantone Solid Matte,

The body shape is drawn as one object; the arms are left out since they are layered above

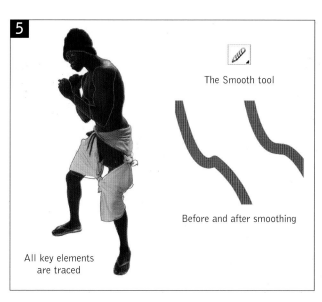

The Smooth tool

Before and after smoothing

All key elements are traced

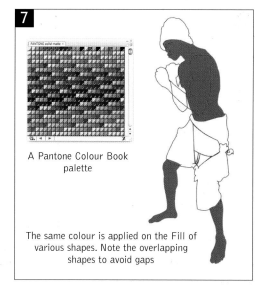

A Pantone Colour Book palette

The same colour is applied on the Fill of various shapes. Note the overlapping shapes to avoid gaps

Illustrator enables you to swap
colours and pattern swatches easily.
Here are a couple of Egle's versions
of her illustration.
Egle Cekanaviciute, Suru 1.

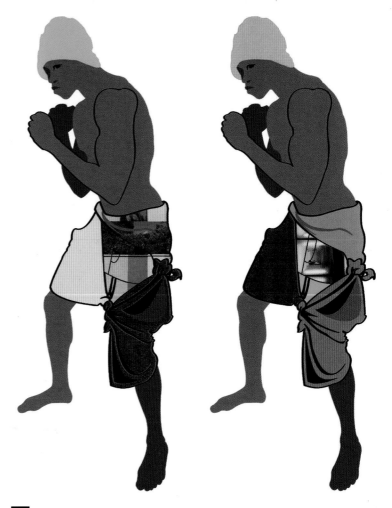

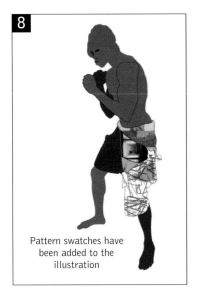

Pattern swatches have
been added to the
illustration

Creases are added to
the garment

for example. (Note that the Pantone Fashion colours are
available on Illustrator but at extra cost). Using the black
arrow, select every element to be filled in the same colour
(pressing ↑ to multiple select). In the colour library click the
desired colour swatch. If you need to colour the Stroke, make
sure that its icon in the Tool palette is in front (same for Fill)
before selecting a colour swatch.

8 Illustrator can use any image (supporting most file formats) as
a pattern swatch and will automatically tile the image when it
is dropped into an object. To create a pattern swatch, start by
opening the picture file in Illustrator, select it and copy paste it
into your illustration file, then drag it into the Swatch palette
(Menu > Window > Swatches). To apply it to a shape, do the
same as with a regular colour.

9 After visualizing your illustration with all its colours you might
want to add some elements, for example creases on the
garment. To do this fast, create a new layer and hide the layer
containing the garments so you can directly see the template
image to trace the new elements.

10 Illustrator's Paintbrush is a fantastic tool, which is discussed
in detail in Chapter 7. But as a first quick-and-easy way to
apply Brush on any object, try this: select a shape with a stroke
colour (in this case the left arm). Go to Menu > Window >
Brush Libraries > Artistic > Artistic Calligraphic, for example.
In the Brush Library palette select a desired brush (make sure
the Stroke icon is in front in the Tool palette). Quite often
brushes are too thick; if this is the case, simply reduce the
stroke weight in the Stroke palette.

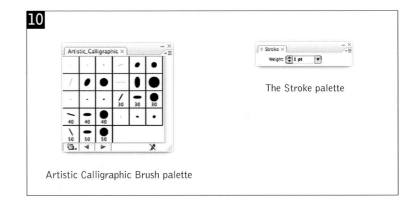

The Stroke palette

Artistic Calligraphic Brush palette

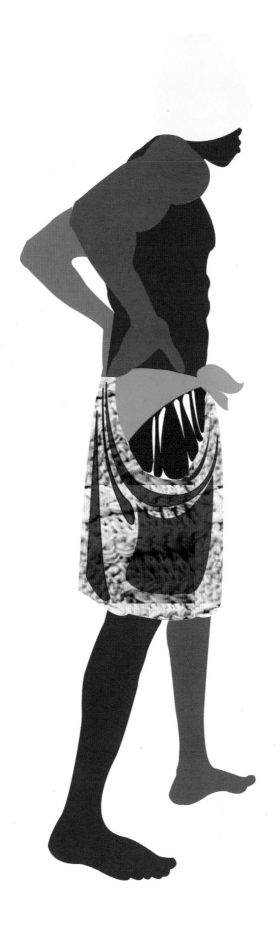

Egle Cekanaviciute,
Suru 2.
Illustrator

Although Mia's illustrations were created in Photoshop using the Lasso and Brush tool, the look is reminiscent of vector illustration and could have been as well produced in Illustrator.

Mia Overgaard,
Unmask me.
Photoshop

Mia Overgaard,
Unmask me II.
Photoshop

Cybèle,
Lolita.
Illustrator

Cybèle,
Layers.
Illustrator

Cybèle,
On the Street, No. 1.
Illustrator

Cybèle,
On the Street, No. 2.
Illustrator

Tutorial 2:

Vector tracing with the Pen tool

Illustrator's Pen tool is less instinctive to use than the Pencil tool, nevertheless, it enables much more control over the drawing of curved and straight lines. The learning curve for the Pen tool is steeper, and for those who have never used this tool before, I recommend practising drawing a succession of straight lines and curves as explained in the tutorial's first step. For those who know the Pen tool already, move to step 2 right away. For further knowledge in vector tracing, this tutorial looks at more in-depth features such as retouching and altering traced vectors; the illustration's background is designed with Illustrator's Symbols.

1 If it is the first time you are using the Pen tool, try to practise with it before tracing an illustration. Select the Pen tool. On the art board, start with a single click to drop the first anchor point. Move the Pen away towards a second anchor point location and click again; a segment is created between both anchor points. Move again to a third location, then press and drag, creating a

Bezier curve, move the mouse around to experiment with the Bezier curve. Release the button to confirm. Finish by going back to the first anchor point, hover over it until you see a small circle next to the Pen-tool cursor, then click to close the object.

2 This tutorial uses a scanned freehand sketch as a template. You do not need to clean up the scan but try to work on the Levels in Photoshop, especially if it is a pencil drawing, to get a good contrast. As in the first tutorial, open the scanned image, lock the first layer, then create a new one.

3 With the Pen tool, start by tracing the outline of the silhouette – use a bright colour Stroke and no Fill. If there are cutouts within the silhouette (such as the gap between the right arm and the body on this illustration), trace them as separate objects. With the black arrow select the main silhouette and the cutout shape (make sure the silhouette has a colour fill), then go to Menu > Window > Pathfinder. In Pathfinder click on the Exclude Overlapping Shape button. This will punch a hole through the silhouette. All design details inside the silhouette

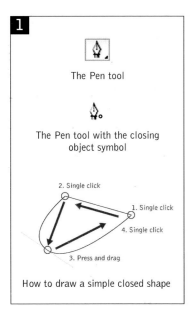

The Pen tool

The Pen tool with the closing object symbol

2. Single click
1. Single click
4. Single click
3. Press and drag

How to draw a simple closed shape

The freehand scanned image

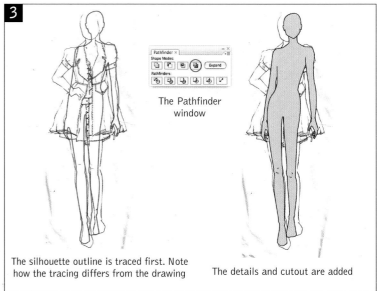

The Pathfinder window

The silhouette outline is traced first. Note how the tracing differs from the drawing

The details and cutout are added

should be added on a separate layer. Don't hesitate to alter the tracing of the original sketch to achieve a better silhouette.

4 Use the white arrow to retouch any bump or unsightly lines by selecting individual anchor points or Bezier handles – imply press and drag anchor points. To create curves where there are none, use the Convert Anchor Point tool (embedded with the Pen tool), or press and drag the anchor point. Use the Reshape tool (embedded with the Scale tool) to reshape segments (press and drag the segment). Reshaping is an important stage, so print out the silhouette to check more accurately any problems.

5 Create a new layer to trace the garment outlines, working in a similar fashion to the silhouette and tracing the outer most edge of the garment. Make sure you close the shape to ensure smooth colouring. Each piece of garment should be on a different layer. Start with garments below. Once the outlines are done, create a new layer for the garment details.

6 Next comes the topstitching, for which Illustrator has dedicated timesaving functions. Create a new layer and with the Pen tool draw any topstitch lines that are not parallel to an edge. Make sure there is no Fill colour; in the Stroke palette, tick Dash Line (if you cannot see this, click on the pop-up menu and select Show Options). The best setting is usually 0.5pt, Dash 1.5 with Round Cap and Join selected (see picture).

7 For stitch lines running parallel along edges or cut lines do as follows: in the layer where the edge line to be topstitched is, select with the white arrow every anchor point within the stitching area. Copy the selection. Go back to the Topstitch layer, paste in front (⌘ + F or Ctrl + F for Windows PC). In the

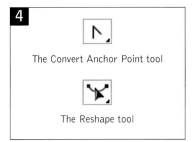

The Convert Anchor Point tool

The Reshape tool

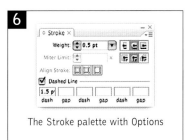

The Stroke palette with Options

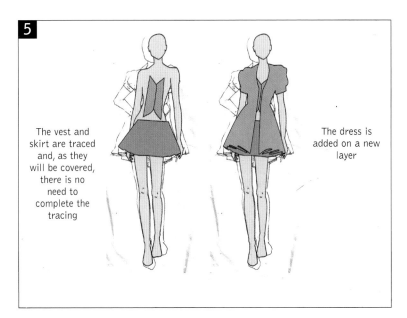

The vest and skirt are traced and, as they will be covered, there is no need to complete the tracing

The dress is added on a new layer

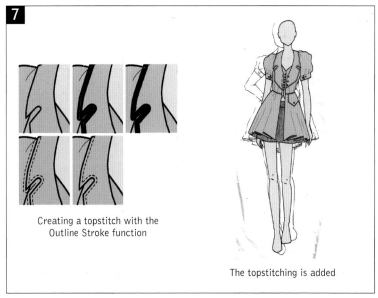

Creating a topstitch with the Outline Stroke function

The topstitching is added

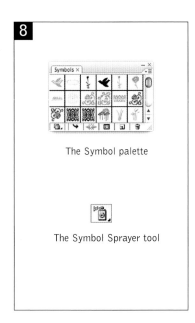

The Symbol palette

The Symbol Sprayer tool

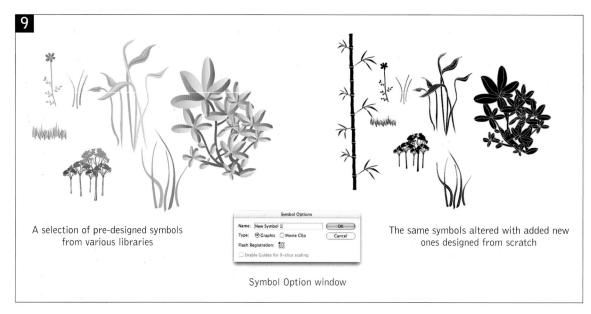

A selection of pre-designed symbols
from various libraries

Symbol Option window

The same symbols altered with added new
ones designed from scratch

Stroke palette input 4pt in the Weight field. (The edge of the Stroke will become the topstitch line so change the value if you want a stitch to be closer or further away.) Go to Menu > Object > Path > Outline Stroke. Set Stroke to Black and Fill to None; select Dash Line. Finish by clearing off the unwanted topstitch line, using the white arrow and Delete key.

8 The background design can be developed using Illustrator's symbols, which are easily reusable 'clipart' objects. Once created or opened you can add multiple instances of a symbol on the art board with the Symbol Sprayer tool or simply press and drag from the Symbol palette. Once applied, symbols can be manipulated (rotation, scale, spacing, etc.) using various dedicated tools embedded within the Symbol Sprayer tool. For this tutorial, pre-designed symbols have been customized.

9 Select various symbols you fancy using for the illustration's background (Menu > Window > Symbol Libraries). Press and drag each symbol on to the art board. Select all the symbols with the black arrow, go to Menu > Object > Expand and press

OK. Then ungroup all the expanded Symbols (⇧+ ⌘ + U or ⇧ + Ctrl + U for Windows PC). You can now change the colour, size and shape of the objects. Finish by dragging them back one by one into the Symbol palette (select Graphic in the Symbol Option window).

10 You can either drop the symbols one by one or quickly duplicate them to compose the background or you can use the Symbol Sprayer tool. Usually the smaller and more numerous the symbols (grass in illustration) the better for the Symbol Sprayer. Bigger and fewer elements (like the bamboos in the illustration) can be manually dropped, scaled and rotated.

Jemma French, Untitled. Jemma's illustrative style works well for a clear representation of garments flat-drawings on a dummy, giving a good idea of proportion and volume. The background adds a mood to the collection.

Pia Bleiht Kristiansen,
Sketchafanne.
Ilustrator

Nice Lopes,
Hat.
Pencil, Corel Draw, Illustrator

Nice Lopes,
Red.
Pencil, Corel Draw, Illustrator

'Most of my work is developed on computer. I use photographic references to observe the face and body dimensions before initiating the production of my illustrations. I like to mix freehand drawings with vector images. The freehand drawings are scanned using Photoshop and turned into vectors in Corel Draw. I use the Freehand tool to start tracing the illustrations. The Form tool helps me with contours. I love playing with colours and trying different combinations to get a surprising result. I'm always looking to mix different styles to create something new.' Nice Lopes

Nice Lopes,
Dress.
Pencil, Corel Draw, Illustrator

Nice Lopes,
Spiral.
Pencil, Corel Draw, Illustrator

Nice Lopes,
Untitled.
Pencil, Corel Draw, Illustrator

Although created in Photoshop, Jamie's illustrations have a distinctive vector look and feel about them, proving that not only Illustrator can deliver such visual aesthetics.

Jamie Cullen,
Stiletto.
Photoshop

Jamie Cullen,
So Me.
Photoshop

Chapter 5
Photographic fashion illustration

At its core, fashion illustration is a drawing depicting garments worn by a model, conveying a look, feel and mood. Fashion photography does exactly the same. Most recently, with the advancement of technology and constant innovation by fashion illustrators, a new kind of fashion illustration is arising, using photography at its core, not simply to be traced and discarded but to be an integral part of the finished illustration.

The creation of illustrations based on photography is possible today thanks to higher computer power and development in applications. Photographic fashion illustration as showcased in this chapter is specifically about how to prepare and transform an original picture using filters in Photoshop or Live Trace in Illustrator. It is interesting to note that even if the original picture is a quite standard snapshot, it can still be made into a beautiful illustration, which enables anyone with a half-decent digital camera and a bit of creativity to produce great fashion illustrations. Mock up a garment in toile, take a picture of it on a model and transform it to make the garment more abstract yet directional to convey a collection's mood: this is the kind of scenario that will be encountered in this chapter.

Tutorial highlights

Tutorial 1
The first tutorial explains the basics of working with photography and centres on a simple Photoshop manipulation using filters and selection tools.

Tutorial 2
The second tutorial looks at Illustrator's Live Trace function using fashion photography as a source. You will also learn how to prepare the picture in Photoshop and how best to customize Live Trace for specific needs.

Key skills:	Application:	Key tools:	Key menu functions:
Working with photography to develop illustration Using Photoshop filters using Live Trace Applying images to vector objects Paths (Photoshop)	Illustrator (AI) Photoshop (PS)	Pen tool (AI) Pencil tool (AI) Smooth tool (AI) Paint Bucket (PS) Crop tool (PS) Magnetic Lasso tool (PS)	Menu > Object > Live Trace (AI) Menu > Select > Refine Edge (PS) Menu > Select > Inverse (PS) Menu > Filter > Filter Gallery (PS CS2 and above only)

Enis Maksutovski,
Trip to New York.
Digital photography, Photoshop

Am I Collective,
Pezula magazine cover.
Photographer: Gerda Genis.
Photography, pen and ink,
Photoshop

Katharina Gschwendtner,
Wald.
Photographer: Dirk Messner,
Deutsch magazine.
Pen and ink, photography,
Photoshop

Tutorial 1:

Photographic illustration with Photoshop Filters

This first tutorial starts with a nice snapshot photograph taken by Shaun Samson for a project with Paul Smith. By using Photoshop Filters smartly, the picture is transformed into an illustration. For this tutorial only two filters are used to produce great results, namely the Cutout and Glowing Edges filters. Interestingly, the selection of what is filtered and what is not gives more depth to the illustration; some solid colour and some detailed photographic features produce a richer visual language.

1 Begin by taking a picture with a clear background, streamlined composition and garment colours to facilitate the filter process. Open the picture in Photoshop and select the Magnetic Lasso tool (especially if the background is clearly different from the subject).

2 The Magnetic Lasso tool works by 'sticking magnetically' to pixels of similar colour. To operate it, position it on the edge of the subject of the picture and single click to begin the process (in this case selecting the garment only), but avoid starting in difficult selection areas such as hair or where the subject colour is close to the background colour. Run slowly along the edge of the subject and single click to drop an anchor point at a key stage (for example before encountering a difficult area). Finish by closing the selection shape.

3 If the Magnetic Lasso failed to select or selected unwanted areas, use the Lasso tool to add or subtract to the selection (Pressing ↑ or Alt). Use Refine Edge (CS3 only) to preview and adjust your selection (⌘ + Alt + R or Ctrl + Alt + R for Windows PC). Once the selection is done, invert it: ⌘ + ↑ + I (or Ctrl + ↑ + I for Windows PC). This selects everything except the original selection.

4 To preserve this selection and be able to reload it whenever you want without having to painstakingly trace it again, you can transform a selection into a path. Make sure the selection is

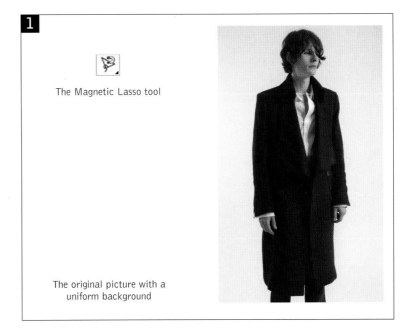

The Magnetic Lasso tool

The original picture with a
uniform background

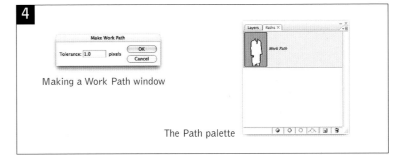

Making a Work Path window

The Path palette

still active, go to Menu > Window > Path; in the Path palette click on the pop-up menu and select Make Work Path, input a tolerance of 1 pixel. In the pop-up menu select Save Path. In the pop-up menu click on Make Selection to transform the path into an active selection.

5 Duplicate the Background layer before applying any filter, enabling you to keep a safe copy of the original picture and try out different filters later. It's worth doing this even if

5

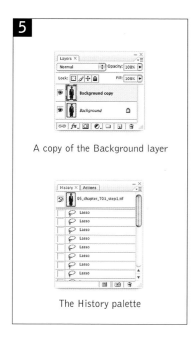

A copy of the Background layer

The History palette

6

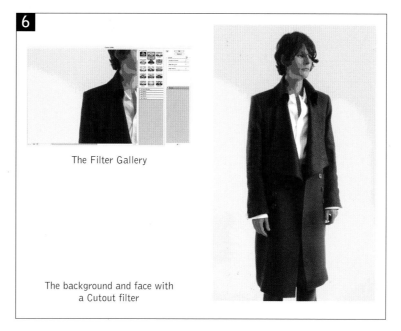

The Filter Gallery

The background and face with
a Cutout filter

7

The background is filled
with solid colour

■ Quick tip

You can also retain selections to be reused at a later stage as
follows: once the selection is made using any selection tool such
as the Lasso or Magic Wand, copy and paste the selection into a
new layer. Don't forget to use the Refine Edge function before
this. Then reload the selection by pressing ⌘ (or Control for
Windows PC) while clicking on the Layer thumbnail (where the
image is).

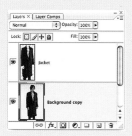

A layer containing a
selected item only

Photoshop's History palette can step back in time; it is still
limited by the number of history states defined (default 20
states) in the Preference panel (Menu > Photoshop (Edit for
Windows PC) > Preference > Performance).

6 To apply a filter on the selection, go to Menu > Filter > Filter
Gallery (CS2 and above only). Select a filter from the menu and
check how it affects the selection in the preview window. To
adjust the filter, experiment with the various sliders found on the
right-hand side. For this illustration the Artistic > Cutout filter
is used with sliders adjusted to Number Level = 7, Edge
Simplicity = 3, Edge Fidelity = 2.

7 With the Background still selected, pick the Paint Bucket tool,
select a foreground colour by clicking on the Foreground Colour
icon in the Tool palette and then click on the background area
around the subject to fill it in. Note how the Paint Bucket only
fills an area with the same colour range (in this case not filling
over the model's head, for example).

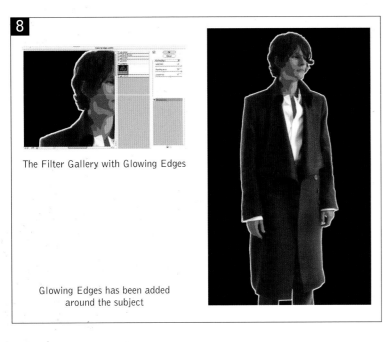

The Filter Gallery with Glowing Edges

Glowing Edges has been added
around the subject

8   Again making sure that the Background is selected, go to Menu
> Filter > Filter Gallery (CS2 and above only), select Stylize in
the menu then select Glowing Edges. Adjust the sliders to try
out the filter's scope and experiment with what is visually
interesting. Press OK to confirm.

9   The illustration is cropped, giving it less of a 'look book'
snapshot feel and more of an illustrative style. Experiment with
different crops to get the right garment details to illustrative
style ratio.

10   Save the illustration, then Save As (⌘ + ↑ + S or Ctrl + ↑ + S
for Windows PC) using a different file name to distinguish it
from the first one. Discard the duplicated Background layer and
duplicate again the original Background layer, then transform
the Path into a selection to start a new filtering process.

Cropping the illustration

Shaun Samson,
Paul Smith Project.
Photography, Photoshop

Katharina Gschwendtner, Prinzessin.
Photographer: Gulliver Theis,
Page magazine.
Pen and ink, photography,
Photoshop

Katharina Gschwendtner,
Krake.
Photographer: Dirk Messner,
Deutsch magazine.
Pen and ink, photography,
Photoshop

Katharina Gschwendtner,
Qualle.
Photographer: Dirk Messner,
Deutsch magazine.
Pen and ink, photography,
Photoshop

Cary Kwok's illustrations are a
perfect blend of digital imagery,
Photoshop compositing and
smoothing filters.

Cary Kwok,
for Barbara Habig 2
Photography, Photoshop

Cary Kwok,
Raphael.
Photography, Photoshop

Cary Kwok,
for Barbara Habig.
Photography, Photoshop

Cary Kwok,
for Barbara Habig.
Photography, Photoshop

Tutorial 2

Photographic illustration with Live Trace

Illustrator, since CS2, has gained with Live Trace a key new function, which supersedes and replaces the long-lost Adobe Streamline. (This tutorial is only relevant for Illustrator CS2 and above.) Live Trace automatically traces bitmap images into vector graphics, thus doing away with the dull and laborious tracing process. This tutorial showcases the creative potential and the pitfalls of Live Trace. Live Trace offers a wide range of creative possibilities for a fashion illustrator, using either preset Live Traces or fine-tuning your own tracing parameters. As in the previous tutorial, Live Trace will require a source bitmap image from which to work; how this image is composed greatly affects the potential Live Trace outcome.

1 Begin by sourcing an image or, better still, composing and styling a shoot. Remember the basics: Live Tracing works best with a plain background, well-defined lines and simple shapes. If you are working from an image sourced on the web, you can retouch it to simplify the background or knock it off altogether.

2 In Photoshop, begin by clearing off any unwanted background elements. Refer to Tutorial 4 in Chapter 1, which described how to work with the Healing Brush and Clone Stamp tools. For the tutorial's photography, the lower left and right corner of the background are doctored away to streamline the look and feel. Remember to duplicate the Background layer to keep a safe copy of the original image in the document. Note that since the picture will be Live Traced, you do not need to spend too much time clearing up the background. A quick, rough retouching should suffice.

3 Take a good look at your image and identify the key elements you wish to highlight. What is your tracing composition going to be like? Are you planning to go for simple, solid colours all over or do you want to have different treatments for different areas? This stage should be considered carefully as it will save time later. In the illustration, the collar, hood, cap and face are most important; the

The original picture

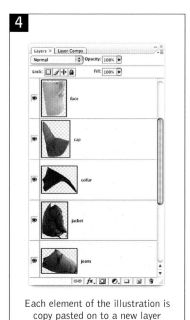

The background is streamlined

The main features are art directed before the post-production process

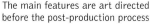

Each element of the illustration is copy pasted on to a new layer

jacket will be streamlined and the background treated separately.

4 Each element of the picture should be separated into a different layer. This enables a much easier and controllable Live Trace process in Illustrator later on. With the Magnetic Lasso tool select each area and copy paste it into a new layer. As with the clean-up step, you do not need to be too accurate since the picture is destined for Live Tracing.

5 Check for any gaps between different layers by hiding the Background (click on the Eye icon) and its duplicate layer. If any gaps or overlaps are in evidence, simply select the faulty layer's content, add to or remove from the selection using the Lasso tool, then select the Duplicate Background layer and copy paste again. Finish by deleting the faulty layer.

6 The picture is now ready for the Live Trace operation. Save the document in Photoshop format. Open it in Illustrator and in the

Photoshop Import Option window select Convert Photoshop Layers to Objects. Each layer of the Photoshop file is imported with the document.

7 The Live Trace function works in two steps: first, tracing; second, expanding. The first steps enable you to preview the tracing before committing to it; the second step transforms the imported image into vectors. This process is destructive, i.e. it deletes the original image. To avoid losing the original image, duplicate all the layers, this will be useful at a later stage when using Blending modes.

8 To Live Trace do as follows: select one of the objects with the black arrow, then in the Control palette select the pop-down menu. Listed are various presets – select one of them, see how this looks and, if you like what you see, press in the Control palette on the Expand button. If you want more control over the tracing select Tracing Options and tick Preview to see how inputting different values affects the image.

5

Some gaps between each element are visible

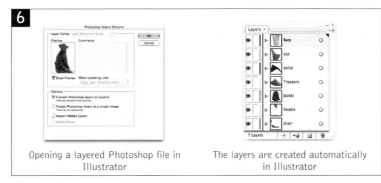

6

Opening a layered Photoshop file in Illustrator

The layers are created automatically in Illustrator

7

The first tracing step

The second tracing step

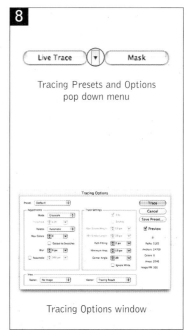

8

Tracing Presets and Options pop down menu

Tracing Options window

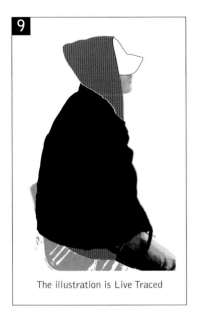

The illustration is Live Traced

■ Quick tip

Live Tracing can create complex vector objects with thousands of anchor points, and the task of retouching these expanded objects can be quite daunting. Use the Outline Viewing mode (⌘ + Y or Ctrl + Y for Windows PC) to view your illustration without any colour fill and strokes for retouching.

The Transparency palette

9 The illustration's various elements are treated with different tracing presets; the preparatory work in Photoshop is paying off, enabling more control over the Live Tracing. After expanding each tracing, retouch it manually, if necessary using the white arrow. Note that, quite often, a white bounding box area is created in the Expand process; this can be deleted with the white arrow by selecting it carefully and pressing Delete. Make sure you ungroup the expanded tracing first (⌘ + ↑ + G or ↑ + Ctrl + G for Windows PC).

10 To finish the illustration, a few Blending modes are added by revealing some of the non-traced images in the layers then selecting different Blending modes or setting a transparency below 100 per cent in the Transparency palette. The background is traced manually and has Gradient fills added.

Original photography David Boulogne, illustration Kevin Tallon

Kevin Tallon,
background image Davide Cimma,
Untitled.
Illustrator, Photoshop

Neil Duerden,
Medieval Medley (left and right).
Photographer: Michael Creagh.
Photography, hand-rendered
sketches/paint strokes, Illustrator,
Photoshop.
Both pieces were the forerunners to
the Westwood Set.

Neil Duerden,
Westwood Couture (left and right).
Photographer: James Lightbown;
model: Alexia Rochford @ Boss;
stylist: Cat Watson;
hair and make-up: Sara Aziz;
clothing: Vivienne Westwood.
Photography, hand-rendered
sketches/paint strokes,
Illustrator, Photoshop

Chapter 6
Mixed-media illustrations

Mixed-media fashion illustrations bring together digitally 'composited' freehand drawings, photography and vector graphics in Photoshop or Illustrator.

Like photographic illustration, recent technological innovations in computer power and software development have enabled this illustrative genre to grow. The increasing size of computer memory and hard drives allows digital illustrators, working on mid-range laptops, to develop content that not so long ago required expensive high-end professional equipment.

Readily available and more affordable digital tools have led to a major boom in mixed-media fashion illustration. Creatively, mixed-media illustration comes in endless combinations and variations: photography with freehand drawing, digital collage of various media, freehand illustration with photographic elements, vector graphics with freehand elements, etc.

The technical skills required to create mixed-media illustrations range from easy to highly advanced and reflect the variety of fashion illustration styles.

Tutorial highlights

Tutorial 1
This tutorial looks at digital collage, from sourcing imagery to layout compositing. Working in both Photoshop and Illustrator, the tutorial highlights differences between both applications and suggests which one is best suited for specific tasks.

Key skills:	Application:	Key tools:	Key menu functions:
Digital collage	Illustrator (AI)	Brush tool (PS)	Clipping mask
Cleaning up a scanned	Photoshop (PS)	Magic Wand (PS)	Menu > View > Actual Pixel (PS)
magazine image		Polygonal Lasso (PS)	Menu > Filter > Blur > Gaussian Blur (PS)
Basic Channel operation			Menu > Filter Sharpen > Unsharp Mask (PS)
Seamless workflow between			Menu > File > Export (AI)
Illustrator and Photoshop			Menu > Window > Channels (PS)
Organizing layers (PS)			

Maren Esdar,
Night-dreams,
Jewels, Fashion and Watches
magazine.
Collage, Photoshop

Enis Maksutovski,
Funky Fall.
Digital photography,
Photoshop, Illustrator

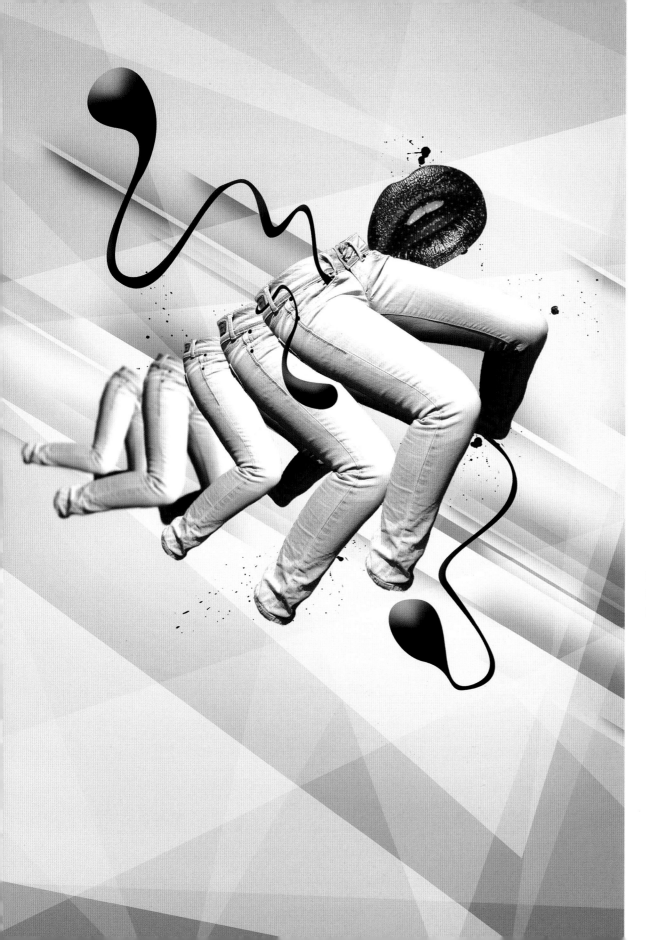

Enis Maksutovski,
Unveiling Love.
Digital photography, Photoshop

Gabriella Bianca,
Chloé Bags.
Mixed-media, Photoshop

Gabriella Bianca,
Equinox.
Mixed-media Photoshop

Mia Overgaard,
Red and White.
Jacket by Comme des Garçons.
Pencil, Photoshop

Mia Overgaard,
Flower Girl.
Pencil, Photoshop

Tutorial 1

Compositing: digital collage

For this illustration, created by Binia Umland, much of the process is actually focused on sourcing image clips to compose the collage. Photoshop will be used to prepare the different clips and, for post-production, Illustrator is used to compose the illustration because its handling of bitmap images permits greater on-the-fly manipulation (such as rotation and scaling).

1 Digital collage sourced from magazines can be prepared before scanning in two distinctive ways, either by cutting clips manually with a good old pair of scissors or by scanning entire pages. If images are sourced from the web, look out for high-quality pictures on file-sharing sites such as Flickr. Try to collect more images than needed to give you more scope for experimentation.

2 The images used for this digital collage are all sourced from fashion magazines; one drawback of using magazines is the inherent four-colour press raster screen, which produces a distinctive 'speckled' look on the paper. To see this close up go to: Menu > View > Actual Pixels.

3 When scanning a magazine, try to scan at twice your output resolution (i.e. 600dpi for a 300dpi print). Start by duplicating the Background layer, then go to Menu > Filter > Blur > Gaussian Blur and input a very low value such as 0.5 or 0.7. Then reduce the image pixel size by a small amount, say from 2,500 pixels to 2,300. Repeat the blur and the image size reduction a couple more times until the screen noise is gone. Finish by using Menu > Filter Sharpen > Unsharp Mask.

4 For more control, you can also apply Gaussian Blur on individual channels, which are greyscale images that store different colour information. An RGB image has a channel for

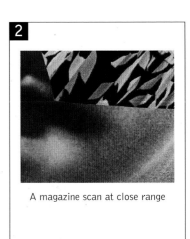

The various scanned clips

A magazine scan at close range

Gaussian Blur

After the Gaussian Blur and the Unsharp Mask

■ Quick tip

Make sure that if you source your clips from a variety of magazines, especially older ones, you scan and apply Gaussian Blur/Unsharp Mask on each clip individually, since they will require a different kind of processing depending on the magazine's print quality.

each colour (red, green and blue) plus a composite channel used for editing the image. To apply Gaussian Blur on, for example, the blue channel, simply hide the green and red channels in the Channel window.

5 Use the Healing Brush and Clone Stamp tool to get rid of any paper marks, blemishes, folds, etc. Follow with the usual Curves and Levels adjustments. If you have scanned entire pages, use the Polygonal Lasso tool to cut out each piece. If you have more than one piece per scan, copy and paste the selection into new layers. Save the file in PSD format.

6 Switch to Adobe Illustrator and open the Photoshop file, importing all layers (tick Convert Photoshop layers to objects). With the black arrow, move the different parts of the collage into position; note how easy it is to select, rotate, scale and

move elements around. Play around with layer order to see what works best. Illustrator enables you to duplicate the elements swiftly, allowing you to try different combinations.

7 Once the basic collage is sorted out, the post-production process can begin. In Illustrator export the file (Menu > File > Export), select Photoshop then Write Layers to preserve all layers. Open the file in Photoshop. Here, some filtering is added using the Filter Gallery, with filters such as Sketch > Photocopy and Distort > Diffuse Glow. Remember to duplicate layers to preserve the original collage safely.

8 The background is hand-drawn and scanned in, thus accomplishing a true mixed-media illustration. Each element is copy pasted into different layers to enable experimentation with fitting around the model. A simple Multiply blending mode

4

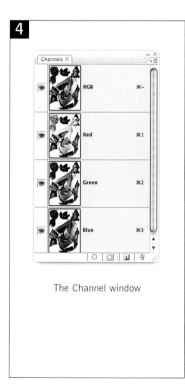

The Channel window

5

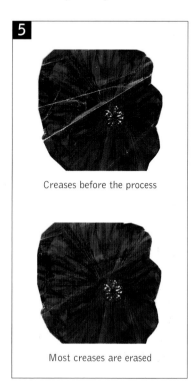

Creases before the process

Most creases are erased

6

The collage is assembled in Illustrator

7

The collage is post-produced in Photoshop

8

The hand-drawn background is added

9

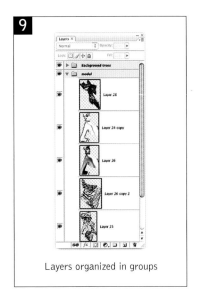

Layers organized in groups

knocks out the white paper background on the tree drawings. The various colouring of the pencil stroke is achieved with the Hue/Saturation function.

9 The last step of compositing will take place in Illustrator using vector graphics for the background. Before saving the file, try to clean up the layers. Quite often when compositing designers create many layers at a fast pace, ending up with a messy layer list. To sort this out use Photoshop's layer folder (click on the Folder icon in the Layer palette) to organize layers in groups. Save the file in PSD format.

10 To give an extra dimension to the illustration, the final composition is created in Illustrator, as follows: open the file as in step 6, lock the layers and create new layers for the vector graphics. Using the Pen tool to draw simple geometric shapes works well in balancing the freehand feel. Solid colours with neat gradients, transparencies and blending modes are added to bring the composition to another level.

Binia Umland,
Model Park.

Maren Esdar,
Antwerp 01,
BOOKLET-Antwerp Special
magazine.
Collage, Photoshop

Maren Esdar,
Pantaloon-dress,
New York Times Magazine – women's
fashion, spring.
Collage and Photoshop

Maren Esdar,
Beauty-extensions,
Avandegarde Magazine.
Collage, Photoshop

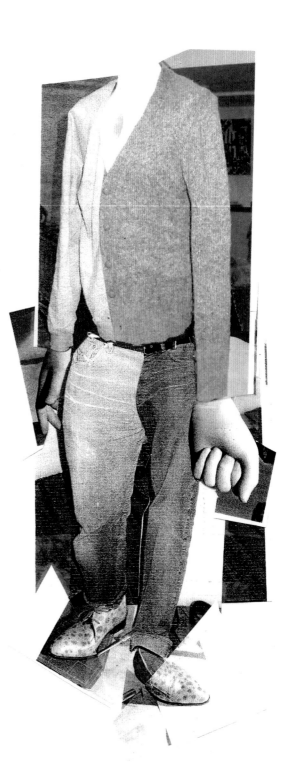

Maximilian Doerr,
Surgery No. 1 (left) and Size
Up/Down (right).
Photography, collage, Photoshop

'I begin by taking black-and-white photos of garments on a model from specific angles. I then distort and cut up the images in Photoshop, playing with scale before printing them out.

I use the printed images to create the whole silhouette, piecing together single garments like jackets, trousers, coat etc. to establish the right look. Next, I add details of garments on top, combined with shoes and accessories.

I would say 80 per cent of my work is done by hand and the other 20 per cent is working with the computer changing proportions. Although proportionally small, the work produced on the computer has a huge impact on the final outcome of the illustration.'
Maximilian Doerr

Maximilian Doerr,
Untitled (both).
Photography, collage, Photoshop

Gerald Moll,
Taurus.
Photographer: Dirk Messner;
styling: Lenn Rosenkranz.
Pencil, photography, Macromedia
Freehand, Photoshop

Gerald Moll,
Sagittarius.
Photographer: Dirk Messner;
styling: Lenn Rosenkranz.
Pencil, photography, Macromedia
Freehand, Photoshop

Chapter 7
Digital painting

Digital painting mimics traditional painting techniques, such as watercolour, oil or airbrushing using digital tools. Digitally painted illustrations are usually entirely created on the computer and, unlike traditional painting, the process is non-linear, meaning that the illustration can be re-edited in various ways without compromising previous steps; thus giving the designer much more choice and freedom for experimentation.

This final chapter covers digital painting for both Photoshop and Illustrator. Each application has very different ways of dealing with digital painting. In Illustrator, the Paintbrush can be applied onto any object or segment and can be changed on the fly. Photoshop uses Paintbrushes more directly and is somehow closer to traditional

painting since once applied the paint stroke cannot be modified. Much like a classic painter would use a model to paint from, digital painting benefits from working with a reference or template. Nevertheless templates in digital painting are more about inspiration and proportion guidance rather than a straightforward template tracing, as showcased in Chapter 4. Any serious designer wanting to create fashion illustrations using digital painting will need a graphics tablet; the mouse is not well suited to applying traditional painting techniques digitally. It is noticeable that in the fashion illustration sector, digital painting is still in its infancy compared to other more mature sectors such as fantasy, animation and classic illustration, which have all fully embraced the genre.

Tutorial highlights

Tutorial 1
The first tutorial focuses on Adobe Illustrator's digital vector painting capabilities, using the Paintbrush tool and a photographic reference template.

Tutorial 2
Digital painting with Photoshop is showcased in this final tutorial, using Paintbrushes to emulate classic painting techniques, but also taking advantage of layers, filters and blending modes.

Key skills:	Application:	Key tools:	Key menu functions:
Digital painting	Illustrator (AI)	Paintbrush tool (AS)	Menu > Object > Expand Appearance
Vector painting	Photoshop (PS)	Paintbrush tool (PS)	Menu > Edit > Define Brush Preset
Working with a graphics tablet		Scissor tool (AI)	Menu > Filter > Brush Strokes > Spatter
Appearance (AI)			Menu > Filter > Blur > Blur More
Creating custom brushes (AI)			Menu > Filter > Noise > Add Noise
Locking transparent pixel (PS)			

Mari Eisl,
Girl.
Photoshop

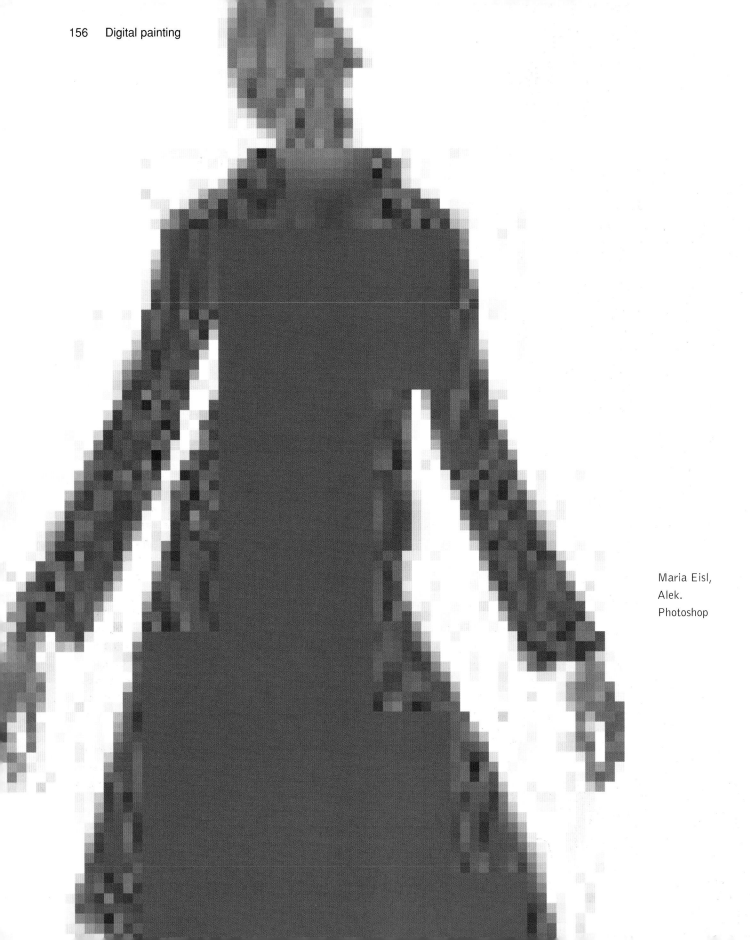

Maria Eisl,
Alek.
Photoshop

Maria Eisl,
Sonia.
Photoshop

Maria uses the qualities of badly
resized or highly compressed jpeg
images to an aesthetic effect. 'The
basis for my illustrations is online
photos from a model-agency
website. I worked on these images
in Photoshop, selecting areas such
as skin, hair and garments, and
painting them in to simplify the
image to its essence: an elegant
model pose.' Down-sizing, heavy
jpeg compression and up-sizing
again enables the jpeg effect to be
highly visible. The gif image format
on the illustration entitled Girl (on
page 155) has other special
qualities that can also be exploited
for digital image-making, such as
layered Photoshop files turning into
animated gifs in ImageReady.

Tutorial 1:

Digital vector painting with Illustrator

Illustrator has over the years grown in dexterity and is now able to challenge Photoshop in the digital painting field, not so much on rendering realistic paintbrush strokes but rather more on paintbrush editing and swapping capabilities. Illustrator's powerful editing capability enables designers to try out different painting styles on the fly. For this tutorial, Denise Paran, using one of her freehand sketches as a template, experiments with Illustrator's Paintbrush tool, including how to edit and swap between various brushes and how to create custom brushes.

1 Start by selecting a suitable template or reference to paint from. If this is the first time you are trying digital painting, opt for a template image or drawing to begin with as this will help with the process; even seasoned users work with

templates. Open the template in Illustrator, lock and create a new layer.

2 A brush stroke in Illustrator is like any other vector object containing segments and anchor points. The difference lies in its appearance, which varies depending on the kind of brush selected (calligraphic, watercolour, charcoal, etc.). The way appearance works enables a quick change of brush style without affecting the underlying segments and anchor points.

3 Painting with brushes in Illustrator is a two-step process: first the segment is drawn, in this case with the Paintbrush tool, but this can also be done with the Pencil, Pen or even a Shape tool. Once the segment is drawn, a Brush can be applied to it (note that if the Paintbrush tool is used a Brush Appearance will be automatically drawn as the segment is painted). For more precision it can be useful to paint using the Pencil tool with a thin line and then apply a Brush to the painted segment.

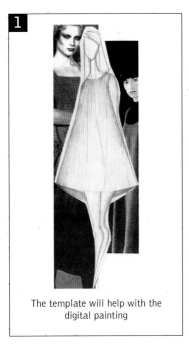

The template will help with the digital painting

A brush stroke with Rough Charcoal Brush applied

The same stroke with Calligraphy Brush applied

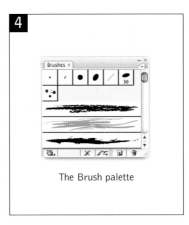

The Paintbrush tool

The Brush palette

■ Quick tip

Remember that digital painting, unlike tracing, only needs a template as a general guide, so let your creativity flow and don't feel hindered by the boundaries of your template. Note how, in this illustration, the legs and hair have been redesigned from scratch to update the original drawing.

4 Start by selecting the Brush tool and in the Brush palette (Menu > Window > Brushes) select a suitable brush; if no brushes appear, select the pop-up menu on the upper right and select Open Brush Library > Artistic Brushes > Artistic Ink (for example). Press and drag across the art board to produce a brush stroke. Experiment with the tool using a graphics tablet.

5 Move on to the template and start painting lines; usually it is easier to start with illustrations containing fewer strokes since brush strokes might need retouching, which can be time consuming. Once your first key lines are placed, use the white arrow to modify parts of the segment or the Reshape tool to modify an entire segment. Try changing the Stroke weight to make the brush thinner or thicker to suit the scale of your illustration or a section of it.

6 You can adjust the sensitivity of the Paintbrush by double clicking on its icon in the Tool palette. This setting is important and needs

to be adjusted to suit your painting style, as the default setting tends to smooth the painted lines too much and can be unnerving when it automatically redraws a painted line too close to the new one (untick Edit Selected Path to undo this).

7 Try out different brushes in different areas. If a brush looks nice on certain portions of a stroke but not on others (especially the endings) you can easily remedy this by cutting the segment where needed as follows: select the stroke with the white arrow and if necessary add an anchor point where the segment needs a cut, then select the Scissor tool. Finish by selecting one or the other part of the segment to give it a different Brush Appearance.

8 Create a new layer and carry on by adding colours to the illustration. To emulate a classic fashion sketch, use fewer bold and flowing paint strokes. Use thick stroke weights to fill in areas quickly and thinner ones where detailing is important. Rather than applying weak paint strokes, thinking they can be altered

5

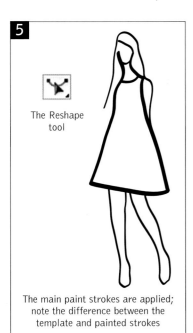

The Reshape tool

The main paint strokes are applied; note the difference between the template and painted strokes

6

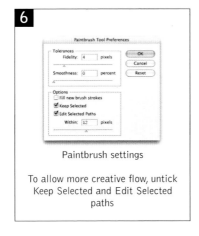

Paintbrush settings

To allow more creative flow, untick Keep Selected and Edit Selected paths

7

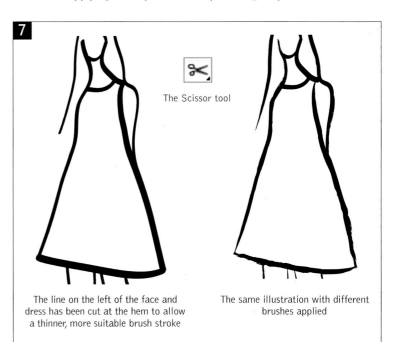

The Scissor tool

The line on the left of the face and dress has been cut at the hem to allow a thinner, more suitable brush stroke

The same illustration with different brushes applied

The finished illustration with added brush strokes and solid-colour shape in the dress; some of the strokes have been expanded and edited as a final touch-up step.

Deniz Paran,
Untitled.
Illustrator

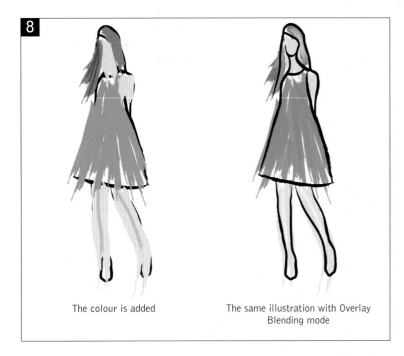

The colour is added

The same illustration with Overlay Blending mode

later, delete them and start afresh. Retouching can be tedious and hinder the desired natural flowing look. To render the natural transparency of ink, select all the colours and in the Transparency palette select Overlay in the Blending Mode pop-up menu.

9 If none of the Art Brushes takes your fancy, you can design a custom brush as follows: draw a shape with any drawing tool (Pen, Pencil, Brush). Select the shape with the black arrow, drag and drop it in the Brushes palette, select New Art Brush in the first window, then in the second one press OK (you can adjust the setting here if needed).

10 Brush strokes can be expanded, meaning they can be transformed into vectors, but once this is done the brush stroke is like any other object in Illustrator and cannot therefore be changed for another brush. To Expand a brush stroke do as follows: select the stroke, go to Menu > Object > Expand Appearance. The brush stroke can then be edited with the white arrow where necessary.

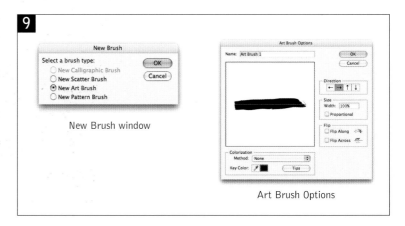

New Brush window

Art Brush Options

Deniz Paran,
Bernhard Willem Fashion Show.
Illustrator

Jen Cox,
Untitled.
Illustrator

Kevin Tallon,
Stroll.
Illustrator

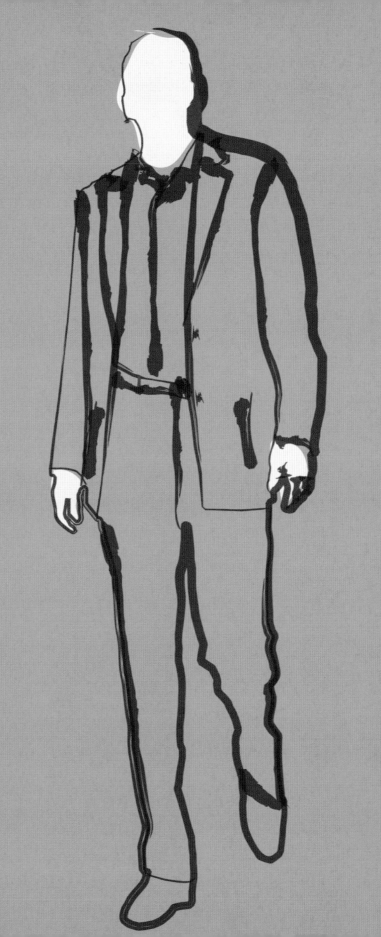

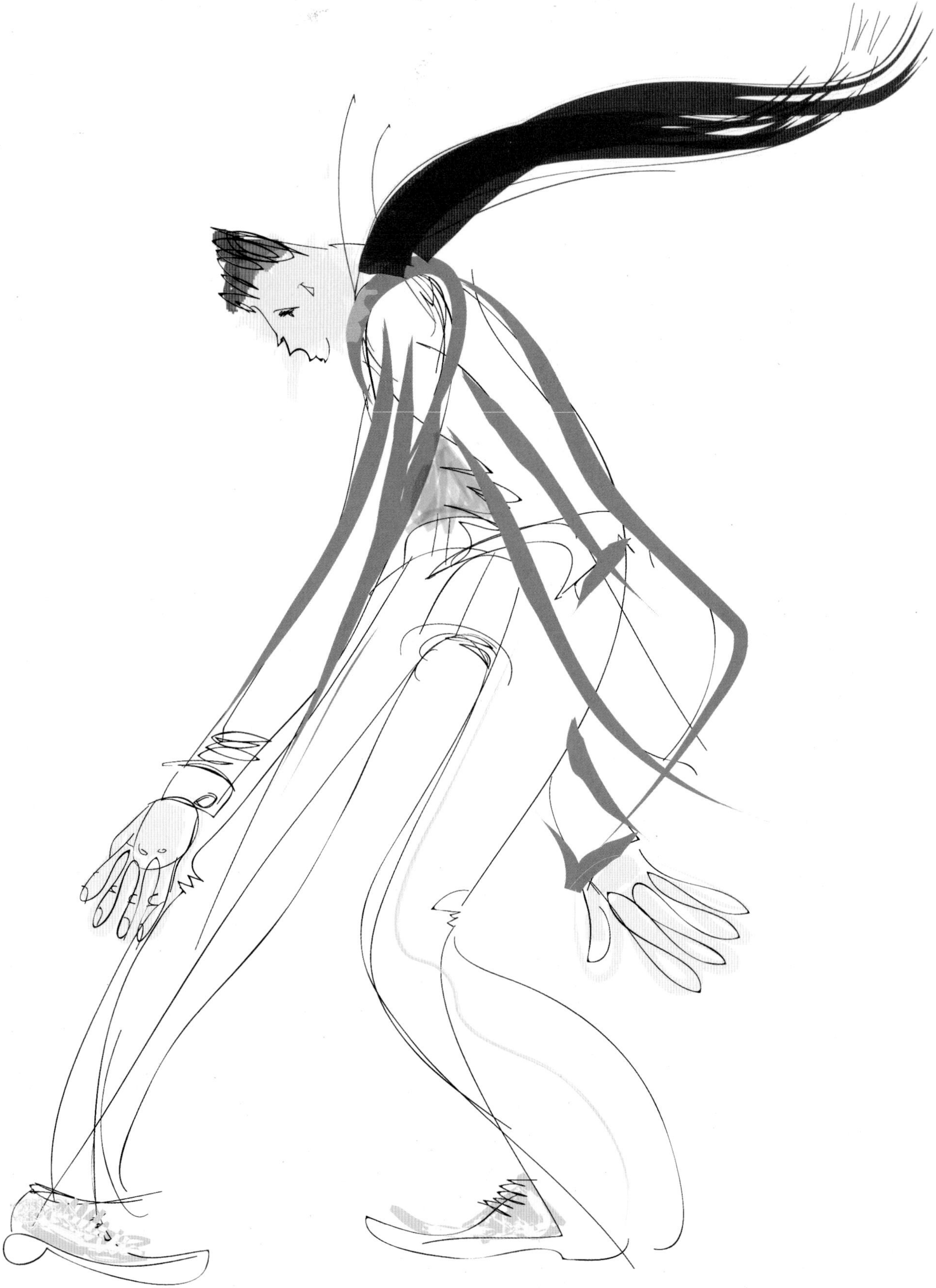

Kevin Tallon,
Monsieur tombe (page 164).
Illustrator

Kevin Tallon,
My Rose.
Illustrator, Photoshop

Tutorial 2

Digital painting with Photoshop

Digital painting with Photoshop is the ultimate 'all-digital' experience, which I hope you will try out. This book started with minimal computer input to finish here with a 100 per cent computer-generated illustration. For this final tutorial mainly pure 'live' painting skills are required. Unlike vector painting, where retouching the segments can be done after applying a paint stroke, Photoshop has no such process, making it trickier and demanding a higher level of digital painting skills. It goes without saying that this is a tutorial that requires a graphics tablet. The artwork developed is based on fashion photography, which really helps, especially if you are a novice digital painter.

1   Start by sourcing a fashion image to use as a template. You can take your own photographs or, as in this case, use an editorial fashion picture. Try to select a picture with a model striking a clear and defined pose; scan in the picture at a high resolution to get as much fine detail as possible. Real images are preferred to achieve realistic highlight and shadows on the skin, but also fabric folds and drape.

2   Before starting the painting, it is important to fine-tune your graphics tablet to enjoy the drawing experience. Tablets come with dedicated driver software enabling customized setting up usually found in the system preference on your computer. Locate the Tablet Driver interface and open it (on a Mac this is found in the System Preferences panel), try out different set-ups, especially the Tip Feel softness or hardness. Try out random brush strokes on a blank canvas to get the feel that suits you. A good graphics tablet is pressure sensitive, as is Photoshop, so try out different pressures when painting.

3   Create a new layer; select a small and hard brush (3–5 pixels, hardness 100 per cent). Set the Opacity and Flow to around 50 per cent. Start the sketching process, using small strokes and

working at close range, trying to produce fast and assured movements rather than slow and shaky ones. This is a first fast sketching process, so don't spend too much time on this; it is primarily to get the main features down on the canvas.

4   Create a white solid filled layer to visualize the illustration better. Develop the habit of hiding the template layer as often as possible to see what your painting progress looks like. Once your first quick sketch is finished, try to go over the main lines with a thicker brush (around 20 pixels). At this point make sure the

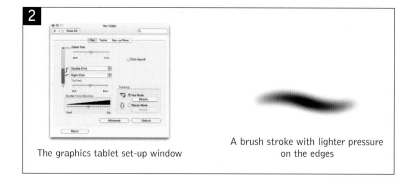

The graphics tablet set-up window

A brush stroke with lighter pressure on the edges

A rough sketch of the illustration is created

The outlines are more refined

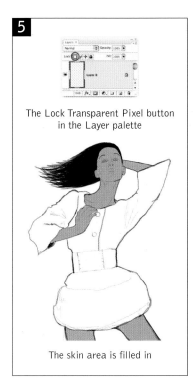

The Lock Transparent Pixel button
in the Layer palette

The skin area is filled in

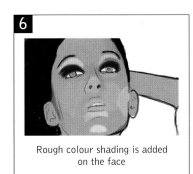

Rough colour shading is added
on the face

The different colour shadings are
blended and smoothed in

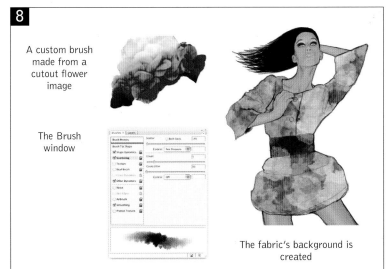

A custom brush
made from a
cutout flower
image

The Brush
window

The fabric's background is
created

template layer is hidden; this is important since you are now really painting your illustration and not tracing any more. Use the stylus eraser by flipping it 180 degrees (just like you would with a regular pencil) to erase any unsightly paint stroke.

5 Next comes the skin painting. Create a new layer; using a bigger hard-edge brush (around 20–30 pixels) with 100 per cent Opacity and Flow and a light colour, paint in the skin areas. You can also use the Lasso tool and the Fill function to work faster. Once the skin is filled in, click on the Lock Transparent Pixel icon, to avoid any spill-over when painting the skin's various shades and details.

6 Drag the template layer on top of the skin layer and then use the Eyedropper tool to select a shade of colour from the template image. Select the skin layer, then, using a soft-edge medium-opacity brush, start by roughly painting the skin's various shades of colour one by one. Hide the template layer to see how your painting looks. I recommend you duplicate the skin layer to have a safe blank copy before starting the shading, as this is quite a tricky process.

7 Follow this by using a soft-edged brush with even lower opacity and flow (10–20 per cent), with which you should blend and fine-tune the various colour shades. Work by gradually building up the paint stroke after stroke (lift the stylus every time you want to add a layer of paint). This process is really quite time consuming but worthwhile to get more depth and subtleties out of your illustration.

8 Next is the dress with a print inspired by Balenciaga's Summer 2008 bold flowers, including oversized hydrangeas, daffodils and anemones. In a new layer, start by painting the fabric's background colour using a 100 per cent opacity hard brush. Continue building the background pattern in a new layer by using a custom brush made from a cutout flower image (Menu > Edit > Define Brush Preset). Before you start painting, open the Brush window (Menu > Window > Brush) and select Pen

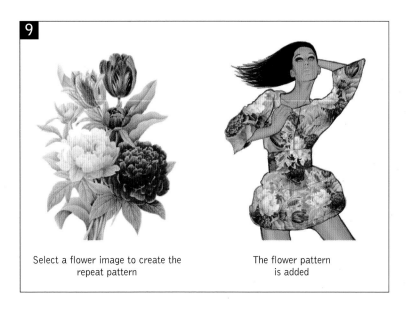

9

Select a flower image to create the
repeat pattern

The flower pattern
is added

pressure in Control then tick on Shape Dynamic, Scattering and
Colour Dynamics. This will make your custom brush react to the
pressure applied when painting, creating random colour,
scattering and shape size. Add a blending mode such as Overlay
to merge the background solid colour and the flowers.

9 Source more pictures of flowers to create the print's repeat
pattern. Using the Lasso tool, knock off the sourced image's
background and then copy paste the flower. Back in your
illustration file, select the fabric background layer's content (right
click on the layer's thumbnail then Select Pixel) then paste into
the flower image (⌘ + ↑ + V or Ctrl + ↑ + V for Windows PC).
Repeat the same operation to add more flowers. Scale and rotate
the flowers to create an interesting repeat print. Select and delete
flowers overlapping fabric cut lines.

10 The illustration is finished by creating a background gradient using
brush strokes rather than the Gradient tool as follows: fill a new
layer with a chosen background colour and then select a wide
(200–300 pixels) and soft brush. With a lighter colour, brush the
gradient highlights from darker to lighter. Make sure the Flow is

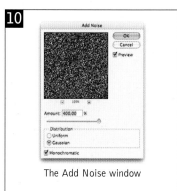

10

The Add Noise window

The finished illustration with added
noise, making it less digitally slick.
Kevin Tallon, Flower Pop.

set to 100 per cent to avoid layering. Because digitally created
illustrations tend to be too 'clean', noise should be added. Fill in
with a shade of mid–grey in a new layer placed on top of all
others, then go to Menu > Filter > Noise > Add Noise; set it to
around 400 per cent, select Gaussian and Monochromatic. Then
go to Menu > Filter > Brush Strokes > Spatter. Finish with
Menu > Filter > Blur > Blur More. Set the layer's Blending
mode to Overlay and adjust Opacity to around 3–6 per cent.

Kevin Tallon,
Raf.
Photoshop

Maria Eisl,
A la folie.
Photoshop

Kevin Tallon,
YSL.
Photoshop

Contributor list

AM I COLLECTIVE
Info@amicollective.com
www.amicollective.com

Gabriella Bianca
info@gabriellabianca.com
www.gabriellabianca.com
Agent for USA: The July
Group, NYC
art@thejulygroup.com
http://www.thejulygroup.com

Pia Bleiht Kristiansen
piableiht@hotmail.com
www.bleiht.com

Lovisa Burfit
www.lovisaburfitt.com

Maria Cardelli
mcardelli-
illustrator@earthlink.net
www.mariacardelli.com

Egle Cekanaviciute
egluzze@yahoo.com

Avigail Claire
avigail@silverspoonattire.com
www.silverspoonattire.com

Jenny Cox
redhotyellowpepper@yahoo.com

Jamie Cullen
www.jamiecullen.net
jamie@jamiecullen.net

Cybèle
www.walkcycle.com

Maximilian Doerr
Maximilian@6in7and8.com

Neil Duderden
www.neilduerden.co.uk
www.unit.nl

Inke Ehmsen
www.inkeehmsen.de
info@inkeehmsen.de

Maria Eisl
m@mariaeisl.com
www.mariaeisl.com

Maren Esdar
Unit CMA
www.unit.nl

Natalie Ferstendik
Represented in UK by
NewDivision www.newdivision.com
Represented worldwide by Unit
CMA www.unit.nl

Jemma French
jjfrench@hotmail.co.uk

Katharina Gschwendtner
kgschwendtner@yahoo.com
www.gschwendtner.info

Ploi Horwang
ploihorwang@gmail.com

Natalie Hughes
natalie.hughes@gmail.com

William Kroll
william.kroll@hotmail.com

Cary Kwok
carykwok@googlemail.com

Eugene Lin
info@eugene-lin.com
www.eugene-lin.com

Nice Lopes
niceaplopes@yahoo.com.br
www.nicelopes.blogspot.com

Enis Maksutovski
hello@ym-germany.de
www.ym-germany.de

Gerald Moll
post@traget-sorge.de
www.geraldmoll.de

Hannah Morrison
london_hannah@yahoo.co.uk

Mia Overgaard
miaovergaard@gmail.com
http://www.miaomiao.dk

Deniz Paran
Deniseparan@hotmail.com

Danny Roberts
dannyroberts@igorandandre.com

Adam Rogers
eyeknowrogers@hotmail.com

Katinka Saltzmann
tinksalt@yahoo.de

Shaun Samson
shaunsantos@yahoo.com

Fredrik Samuelsson
samuelzone@hotmail.com

Kevin Tallon
Kevin@designlaboratory.co.uk

Howard Tangye
h.tangye@csm.arts.ac.uk

Maria Teninzhiyan
mariaten@googlemail.com

Binia Umland
Thetallons@talktalk.net

Pier Wu
lemeutesilente@gmail.com

Neil Young
neilyoung01@hotmail.com

Index